THE GREATEST STORIES

EVER PLAYED

THE GREATEST STORIES

EVER PLAYED

VIDEO GAMES

— and the —

EVOLUTION OF STORYTELLING

DUSTIN HANSEN

FEIWEL AND FRIENDS
New York

A Feiwel and Friends Book
An imprint of Macmillan Publishing Group, LLC
120 Broadway, New York, NY 10271 · fiercereads.com

Our books may be purchased in bulk for promotional, educational, or
business use. Please contact your local bookseller or the Macmillan
Corporate and Premium Sales Department at (800) 221-7945 ext. 5442 or
by email at MacmillanSpecialMarkets@macmillan.com.

Library of Congress Cataloging-in-Publication Data
Names: Hansen, Dustin, author.
Title: The greatest stories ever played : video games and the
evolution of storytelling / Dustin Hansen.
Description: First edition. | New York : Feiwel and Friends, 2022. |
Summary: "A lifelong gamer with over 20-years experience in the
gaming industry examines the storytelling skills in some of the most
beloved and moving games of the past thirty years in this fun and
informative YA non-fiction title"—Provided by publisher.
Identifiers: LCCN 2021025257 | ISBN 9781250183569 (hardcover)
Subjects: LCSH: Video games—Authorship—Juvenile literature. | Video
games—History—Juvenile literature. | Storytelling—Juvenile literature.
Classification: LCC GV1469.34.A97 H36 2022 |
DDC 794.8—dc23/eng/20211020
LC record available at https://lccn.loc.gov/2021025257

First edition, 2022
Book design by Raphael Geroni
Feiwel and Friends logo designed by Filomena Tuosto
Icon graphics © by Incomible/Shutterstock
Drop cap letters © by Yuravector/Shutterstock
Printed in the United States of America

ISBN 978-1-250-18356-9 (hardcover)
1 3 5 7 9 10 8 6 4 2

For Tanner. The world belongs to those who have no fear, eat salty chips, and seek for the wild among the norm. Let's make dangerous things together, that won't soon be forgotten.

TABLE OF CONTENTS

A Note from the Author— Oh, Boy, What Have I Done?

Story (N.)

a: An account of incidents or events;

b: the intrigue or plot of a narrative or dramatic work;

c: what happens when a character faces an unavoidable, challenging obstacle, and how they change because of it.

'VE BEEN WRITING BOOKS FOR A LONG TIME. MORE than fifteen years, I'd guess. And before that, I designed games and wrote professionally for the video game industry. In one way or another, I've been writing or thinking about writing for a quarter of a century. Twenty-five years, at least. That's a long time. Well, at least it is from my perspective.

And during that entire time, this book or a version of it has been playing in the back of my brain. I've written hundreds of thousands of words about story and games that will never be read by another human. I've got a filing cabinet full of notes I've taken while playing games, capturing everything from the emotional impact to the dialogue to the moments that made my jaw drop. I even have notes on the not-so-great games. I don't play favorites when I'm capturing my impressions in the privacy of my own game room.

It is an endeavor, or maybe a journey, that I've been on for half of my time here on earth.

Story is the creative lifeblood that pumps through my heart. But I think you'll agree that story isn't the only thing that makes a game great. There are great games out there that are totally void of story. Not just bad stories, but games without any story whatsoever. Seriously. Games are complex and run the entertainment gamut.

Yet a game with a fantastic, emotional story arc will always hold a special spot in my gamer heart. And a fun game to play, combined with a great story, is a rare gift. It's a marvel something like this can even exist. They're so big and so . . . is *complete* the right word? Considering all the people and countless hours of work that go into making a knockout, blockbuster title, it's incredible when a singular vision with impact gets produced. We truly are living in remarkable times.

A second thing I'd like to point out is that while twenty-five years of studying, playing, reading, and creating stories seems like a long time in a single human's experience, it isn't even a blip on the time line of storytelling history. This might be the biggest issue with storytelling in games, so I want to get it out of the way early. Games are infants in the storytelling world. And babies make mistakes.

If we examine the lifetime of film, which is widely accepted as one of the best storytelling mediums humans have created, we're only looking at around 120 years, give or take a decade. And even that is just a blip on the time line of storytelling history. Compared with movies, games have only been telling stories since the 1970s, and in that time, the rules of how games work have changed considerably. And the delivery devices change dramatically about every five or so years as well.

To put this in perspective, while things have certainly changed in the book world over the last five hundred years, you can still read a William Shakespeare sonnet in basically the same format that Ole Willie, as I like to call him, intended. You can even do a side-by-side comparison of his writing to that of a modern-day poet or playwright. But while it isn't *impossible* to find a working PDP-10 mainframe computer to play the original version of *Colossal Cave Adventure* in its purest form, it isn't the same as playing *Ratchet & Clank: Rift Apart* on your new PlayStation 5. Yeah. To say that things have changed is a monumental understatement.

Screenshot of Will Crowther's original Colossal Cave Adventure running on a Windows computer, next to a screenshot of the PS5 game Ratchet & Clank: Rift Apart © Sony Interactive Entertainment

The speed at which game development and video game story-telling have evolved is unprecedented. In no other time—from prehistoric to modern—have we experienced a change in how we tell and enjoy stories as we have in the last forty years. I don't want to exaggerate too much, but that *is* a big deal. Because stories are a big deal to us. And I don't mean that in the public, universal, objective sense; I mean that stories matter to every individual in a profoundly personal, practical way.

As you might imagine, this type of rapid change can cause a few bumps in the road. Not every game made is going to be a winner, and when a huge portion of the storytelling takes place in a player-controlled environment, there is a lot of room for error. What I'm trying to say is, there's been some bad games.

But the game industry has created masterpieces. Deep, rich, complex, emotional stories that put *you*, the gamer, right in the middle of the conflict and ask you to decide your own fate, or, at the very least, experience it.

I'll fully admit my bias. I love everything about story games. Creating them, playing them, writing about them. And I know I'm preaching to the choir. The majority of people who grab this book are here because they already love story-based games, too. But I'm pretty confident in stating that the most original and innovative storytelling happening now and in the future will take place in the game space.

A foundational element of a great story is that it cries to be shared. That drive to share a story is biological. It was in sharing the stories of man and gods and beasts that ancient societies warned of potential hazards. The cautionary tale. Of course, not all games are cautionary tales, and to show my bias once again, I personally think that video games are the most shareable of media. So much, in fact, that entire platforms like Twitch have staked their future in gamers streaming and talking about how the games we play affect our lives. And they aren't going anywhere anytime soon (fingers crossed).

I'm willing to bet that all of us who have experienced the power of using a controller to move the story forward rather than turn a page have had that experience where we have to pause, set down the controller, and just think. Or better yet, *feel* for a moment before we can go on. I know I have. And the wonderful thing is that we all bring our own backgrounds and understandings to the games we play. When we mix that with a medium that requires us to actively participate in how the story unfolds, we get this unique, personal attachment that speaks to us in meaningful ways.

For me, if I'm being really honest, that has only happened about a dozen times. Don't get me wrong. I've enjoyed hundreds of good story games, but that special moment I'm talking about is special for a reason. I remember each of these moments because they don't happen very often. They left an indelible mark on my life at the time. It happened the first time I joined a group of fellow travelers in *Journey*, sand-skating peacefully as the setting sun glowed through the massive pillars of an abandoned temple, only to be removed from my new friends and dropped into a lonely, dark abyss. It happened when I struggled through the wrecked interior of a train dangling precariously over a snowy mountain cliff as Nathan Drake in *Uncharted 2: Among Thieves*. And it happened most recently as I escaped the city of Jackson as Ellie, Dina nearby, as we enjoyed a solemn moment in a lush evergreen forest on horseback.

But there's a chance that not all these moments will have the same impact on you as they did on me. As I said, we bring our own experiences to the game, and this changes our perception. It's like if you asked fifty artists to do the same rendition of a hilltop sparsely populated with plant life, no two illustrations would be the same. The term I'm poking around at here is *subjective*. Games aren't alone; every story medium shares the subjectivity phenomena. While we can generally agree that some things are better than others, when it comes down to claiming that something is the greatest of all time, the debate will rage. We'll all be right. We'll all be wrong.

And, really. Isn't that what makes it all so compelling? Remarkable art, and I'll argue that games are exactly that, art, requires a lot from the viewer. It can be both harmonizing and polarizing. It makes us think. It encourages us to share. It makes us disagree. It makes us talk.

Great art makes us feel.

So, gamer, this is where our troubles begin, and it goes like this. You will probably find that at least one, perhaps more, of the games I discuss in this book does not fit *your* criteria for Greatest Games Ever Played. And I can pretty much promise that you'll have a few that you'd like to have on the list that I've left out. In fact, I have a few more *I'd* like to be included. There are so many that could have made the cut, but cuts were made. It's the nature of things. Cuts must always be made.

I did my best to set my personal biases aside and look at the games that we generally agree are the best of the best. But if I'm going to give you the most honest book I can, I have to allow some preferences to soak through. However, this is where you come in.

As you read the book, keep a notebook handy and jot down your thoughts. Your impressions. Places where we agree, and places where we don't. And if you find you have a story that is just begging to be discovered in more detail, I'd love to hear about it. We'll find a way to get in touch. It isn't hard; I'm easy to find online. And I'm not kidding. I want to hear about your favorite games, because there's a good chance I've played them, too. And knowing the game that you love the most will give me an idea of who you are and what *you* bring to the gaming table. And I've found that is a great shortcut to our becoming friends.

But if you have a favorite that I haven't played, well, that's even better. That is where you help me grow. I wouldn't mind adding a few more amazing story games to this list. And hopefully you'll find something inside these pages that will return the favor. A new game or two for you to explore.

All right. Enough. You get it, right? There have been a lot of games. Storytelling in games is, in the grand scheme of things, both new and ever-changing. Because of the nature of story, we are asked to participate and bring our personal experiences to the party, and this, in turn, changes how we respond to the stories we play.

Oh, and one last thing we can all agree on. Games are freaking great at this stuff, and I can't wait to see, or better yet, *play*, what comes next.

Once upon a Time . . .

Immersive (Adj.)

Noting or relating to digital technology or images that actively engage one's senses and may create an altered mental state, occupying most of one's attention, time, or energy.

ATHER AROUND THE CAMPFIRE, GAMERS; I HAVE a story to tell. It goes back quite a bit further than you might think.

Way back past the PlayStation.

Before the Commodore 64 and the Atari 2600.

Years and years before arcade games like *Pong* and *Space Invaders* came on the scene in the 1970s.

Centuries before film, TV, and radio. Heck, even before newspapers. Let's go back to a time before your great-great-great-great-greatest-off-all-greats-grandfather was carving stories on slab tablets with a stone hammer and an old rock chisel.

Back to the beginning. Are you there?

Good. Because this is where it all begins. I'm not kidding. Back before, well just about everything, people were already telling stories. With their barely covered backsides parked on logs, they sat around a campfire, roasting prehistoric marshmallows and listening to tall tales about hunting parties, boulder-throwing contests, and cautionary tales about how porcupines make terrible lapdogs.

Storytelling is a part of who we are as human beings. It's biological. They not only entertain us, they teach us. Stories inspire us, terrify us. They make us laugh and cry. Stories bring us together and show us that even though we are different in many ways, we are all linked through common bonds that resonate deep within us.

And when something is this important, we, as humans, have a desire to write it down. We just can't help ourselves. Our ancestors knew this more than thirty thousand years ago when they painted on the walls of their caves, in what is now called France, murals that told of their greatest adventures.

Around 3200 BC, small pictures called cuneiform were pressed into clay. The clay slabs were fired over hot coals for hours to harden and preserve. These small pictures were the beginnings of written language, but it was the technology of the clay slabs that moved this process forward. Believe it or not, denting notches into clay with a sharp stick, then cooking it until it was as hard as a rock, was a big technological advancement. Yeah, high technology made from mud and fire.

In another couple of hundred years, those early pictures simplified into symbols and letters, and the first books and histories were recorded on less permanent medium. Back then, they hammered reeds and water into a paper called papyrus. And you can image how outdated a backpack full of heavy clay tablets would have seemed if your buddy was walking to school with the new and improved papyrus copy of his schoolbooks. Once again, technology advanced how stories were told. It was easier than ever to record stories, and guess what that meant? It meant more people wanted to learn how to read—and write.

The Industrial Revolution brought us machines capable of pressing lots of high-quality paper on the cheap. No longer did a bookmaker have to smash grass into pulpy sheets on the banks of the Nile River. And while the first books were copied carefully by hand, the basic form of a book really didn't change much for quite some time. In fact, early bookmakers were so brilliant that remnants of their paper and book-printing processes are still used today in books like the one you're holding in your hand. Then newspapers and the printing press came along, and once again, storytelling technologies became more effective.

Now people could write a story on a Saturday and share it with hundreds, even thousands, of people by Sunday afternoon. It changed the way stories were told. Bit by bit. A chapter at a time to keep readers begging for the next installment that would be shared in the following week's newspaper.

Then things got really crazy as stories literally came to us through the air. Radio made its way onto the scene. Talk about a huge leap in technology. Now someone could write a story and an actor could read it into a microphone that day, and it would be shared instantly to everyone within the station's reach.

Television and film took the voices brought to life on radios and matched them with faces and far-off places. Storytelling became passive for the first time, and it was good. *Great* even. No longer did you have to use your imagination, turn pages, and reread difficult passages. You sat there in the dark and the story flooded from the screen to your itchy eyeballs, and it was, and still is, *amazing*!

But what's next? What comes after TV and film? It's a question, believe it or not, that I hear all the time. What technology will move storytelling to a whole new level? And how will we tell stories in the future? Some people think we're done inventing. That we've told stories in every possible manner, and that everything new today is just a reinvention of yesterday. Audiobooks are just radio reinvented. Plays on a stage are nothing more than campfire stories told with costumes and sets and makeup. 3D films? Imax? Nothing new to see here. Those are just big, fancy ways of watching an old black-and-white silent film in the 1920s.

But I don't think we're done yet. Not even close. If the history of storytelling has shown us anything, it's this: People always want more exciting and immersive ways to tell stories. And second, technology and storytelling are linked. Hand in hand, throughout history and on and on forever.

In the next few hundred pages or so, we're going to look at storytelling in the most immediate, interactive, and immersive medium to date.

We're going to look at how story has changed in the last thirty years, and why that is so significant. We'll dig into what binge-watching TV episodes on Netflix has in common with your favorite video game. We'll take a deep dive into how pressing buttons on a PS4 controller is a form of communication. We'll ask ourselves important questions like "Can a video game make you cry?" and "Should you be able to write a book report on a video game?" and maybe even "What does it take to be a writer in the video game industry?"

But most of all, you and I are going to look back at the greatest stories ever played.

A BIT OF FAIR WARNING
BEFORE YOU PROCEED.

THIS IS IT.

YOUR OFFICIAL SPOILER WARNING.

From here on out, as I discuss games, I am going to spoil the pixels out of 'em. For some of these games, in order to talk about what makes their stories so good, I have to talk about the endings or the major plot points.

Uncharted 4:
A Thief's End

Parallel Narrative (N.)

Also referred to as parallel stories or parallel plots, it denotes a story structure in which the writer includes two or more separate narratives linked by a common character, event, or theme.

ROM THE MOMENT HE ARRIVED ON THE VIDEO game scene, Nathan Drake was destined to become a hero. Or, at least, that is what Naughty Dog wanted us to believe. It was 2007 when we were first introduced to *Uncharted* on the PlayStation 3. There's no doubt Naughty Dog was going after the treasure-hunting subgenre *Tomb Raider* created. *Uncharted: Drake's Fortune* was a bit of a sleeper hit, and the series has grown into one of the bestselling franchises of all time. The gameplay, while a bit dated if you go back today, set a standard at the time for 3D platforming and approachable gun mechanics. The talent on display, from the acting to the snappy dialogue to the visuals, felt like a spectacular, big-budget blockbuster where the player controls the hero. Fans loved the superficial, square-jawed, rock-climbing playboy from the start, and by the time the second game was announced, players were itching to get their trigger fingers on the new release.

Uncharted: Drake's Fortune © *Naughty Dog*

In *Uncharted 2: Among Thieves*, fans felt that the PlayStation 3 finally had a game that showcased what the system was capable of. Not only were some of the clunkier aspects of the gameplay from the first *Uncharted* ironed out, but the larger-than-life set pieces, cinematic orchestral soundtrack, and the likable characters also set it apart from all its competition. When the third game in the series, *Uncharted 3: Drake's Deception*, came out, two years before the release of the PlayStation 4, it seemed that the developers had set the bar yet again for what could be achieved visually and cinematically in games.

Uncharted was on a roll. The series seemed unstoppable, and when the PlayStation 4 came out, everyone was hungry for the next offering. Gamers wanted to hang out with their favorite unflappable hero, Nathan Drake, again. But they'd have to wait. Naughty Dog was in the throes of developing another new IP, an intellectual property, called *The Last of Us*, and they wanted to get that game just right before returning to Nate's adventures.

You might be asking yourself why I'm bringing all this up? Why is it important to understand the context surrounding *Uncharted 4*? Part of this is that I believe that understanding the history behind a great work of art makes you appreciate its value more. And it's also good to know the order of these Naughty Dog games, because it helps to see how each game is influenced by the ones that came before. It's particularly interesting to watch a studio learn from their own mistakes. Basically, what I'm saying here is, the five-year break and the work the team did on *The Last of Us* had a major influence on the way Naughty Dog approached *Uncharted 4*'s story, and more important, Nathan's character.

Pop culture has given us characters like Nathan for a century or more. You know the trope of the "good guy" who mows down anyone in his path as he becomes the hero of the story. And rather than shy away from that stereotype, Naughty Dog laid into it with both guns blazing, pun intended. Not only does Nathan Drake shoot first and joke later, but he also does it with an efficiency that is so over the top that we kind of just get used to it. In the first three games, Nathan is charming. He's the rough-cut American version of James Bond. He's funny, he shows no mercy for bad guys, he's smart, and he's got looks that would fit on the silver screen.

In every way, Naughty Dog has encoded him to be a hero, but for some, this happy-go-lucky, winner-takes-all persona is undercut by his brutality and the body count he leaves behind. Look, Nathan Drake is no saint. In fact, to really fall for this guy, you need to push aside the fact that he's killed hundreds, maybe thousands, of baddies, not to mention a few innocent bystanders, along the way. And not only that, but he does all this with a smirk and a witty quip that minimizes the violence.

And while *Uncharted* fans generally loved Drake, Naughty Dog wasn't finished crafting this complex character. And we owe some of that to the time they spent on *The Last of Us*. While the *Uncharted* series to date had been very focused on larger-than-life action sequences and adventurous treasure hunts, *The Last of Us* was a more intimate, character-driven experience.

And after crafting that game, which is widely acclaimed as one of the greatest story games ever told, the team returned to the *Uncharted* world and took it in a new direction by making Nathan Drake more vulnerable and truer to his gameplay narrative. Formerly, Nathan's character was incongruous to his actions because he killed people for gold and fortune, yet he was somehow the good guy. But we're not supposed to like him less for his countless acts of homicide, because he charms us with a debonair shrug and cracks a joke about Sully's fine backside. It's an unspoken agreement between the developers and the audience that *Uncharted* is an action-adventure, Indiana Jones–style blockbuster. That is, until *Uncharted 4: A Thief's End*.

In *Uncharted 4*, Naughty Dog didn't ignore his weaknesses, rather, they shone a light on his inherent selfishness and tried to redeem him despite his flaws. As the game opens, fans of the series are immediately thrown off balance by Nathan's claims that he is finished with treasure hunting. He is back with his wife, Elena Fisher, the woman he fell in love with during his travels, and they are living a quiet, suburban life. Longtime *Uncharted* enthusiasts have always known Nathan to have an unquenchable thirst for adventure, so why the sudden shift in lifestyle?

It seems the most danger Nathan allows himself is to deep-sea dive for cargo. He used to live to break the rules, but now he won't even risk taking a salvage job without the proper permits, even when Elena encourages him to. Strangest of all, it's been years since he last spoke to Victor Sullivan (Sully), one of his oldest partners in crime and a positive role model for him since he was a teenager. It's as if Nathan is an addict practicing abstinence, one who lives every day in fear of relapse, avoiding his vice of lawless adventure.

If you'd played all the games up to this point, you might have guessed why Nathan had agreed to settle into a more mundane life: because of the obvious danger his lifestyle puts him and his loved ones in. Not to mention that he nearly lost Elena because of his pattern of putting adventure and greed above personal relationships. But now, to help players understand this change of heart, the game takes us back to Nate's childhood, time and time again, letting us learn more about what makes him tick.

In a flashback, we learn Nathan and his older brother, Sam, were given up to the state by their father after their mother died. Cassandra's passion was solving mysteries of the past, and her two greatest cases were the quest to discover the location of Captain Henry Avery's stolen treasure and her drive to uncover the heirs of the mysterious Sir Francis Drake. Their father, instead of giving the grieving brothers their deceased mother's research notes, a final, precious memento of her, sold them to a collector and dumped his sons at the doorstep of the St. Francis Boys' Home.

This enlightening, yet painful, memory reveals that Nathan and Sam's passion for adventure is fueled not only by greed but also by a burning desire to connect with the mother they barely knew. Discovering Captain Avery's gold has greater meaning to the brothers than its monetary or historical value. It also became a personal vendetta against the injustice of her passing. This is a much stronger motivation for our hero than he hunts treasure because he likes shiny gold things.

When it comes to storytelling and writing, deepening or strengthening the "why" behind your character's needs makes them more sympathetic. More universal. Sure, we'd love to find some buried treasure, it's why the treasure-hunting genre has been around for centuries. But we can empathize with Nathan's and Sam's motivations here because we have felt similar feelings. We have loved ones in our lives (parents, siblings, friends, mentors) who mean the world to us, and making them proud or living up to their legacy is something very human and much more relatable than rock climbing in Shambhala for gold artifacts.

With the revelation of Nathan's mother's interest in Sir Francis Drake, we begin to understand the motivations for the past adventures Nathan has undertaken, and more emotional weight is added to stories told in the previous games. Nathan's desire for adventure and treasure is linked to his past in a meaningful way, and we learn that he's more complex than we ever thought. Naughty Dog continues to deepen this connection with the character and his history as you play through multiple time lines in Nathan's story.

An unspecified amount of time after being abandoned by their father, Nathan and Sam escape the orphanage and retrieve their mother's research papers from a woman named Evelyn. They change their surnames from Morgan to Drake in honor of their mother's theory that Sir Francis Drake had heirs. And on the spot, they dedicate their lives to finding Captain Avery's treasure by any means necessary. This pact is extremely significant. Not only is it a symbol of the emotional pain they feel and their commitment to resolving it, but it's also key to understanding the major source of conflict in the story.

Later in life, clues lead the brothers to purposefully get incarcerated in a Panamanian jailhouse while on their quest for Avery's gold. As lifelong lawbreakers, getting arrested was the easy part. The difficulty lies in locating a cross with a crucial tip-off about Avery's treasure from within the prison before making their escape. After recovering the artifact, they trigger a jailbreak and try to slip out undetected amid the chaos. Things go horribly wrong when Sam is shot in the back and falls multiple stories, crashing through a corrugated steel roof. Shocked, full of adrenaline, and spurred on by the nearby gunfire, Nathan is forced to leave his beloved brother behind for dead. The hope of discovering Henry Avery's gold and finding closure for the loss of their mother dies with him.

Nathan lost his purpose and his family in a single moment. He couldn't bring himself to continue his search for Avery's treasure alone.

He distracted himself by searching for legendary El Dorado in *Drake's Fortune*, Shambhala in *Among Thieves*, and the lost city of Iram of the Pillars in *Drake's Deception*. But that only tells us why he stopped looking for Avery's treasure. At the beginning of *Uncharted 4: A Thief's End*, he has quit treasure hunting altogether. Why?

The game doesn't spell it out at first, but as we get to know Nathan better, we can start to guess. Perhaps he gave it up because he knew the tiniest temptation of a lost city would be enough to whet his appetite, and once he began investigating, he wouldn't be able to stop until he found it. Maybe he left because fortune seeking caused old wounds to emerge, and it became easier to live with the dull pain of lost loved ones as time passed. Or, as I suggested earlier, maybe he quit because of the danger it put his friends in. Or he could have quit because he truly appreciated the value of his relationship with Elena and finally understood that lasting happiness does not come from riches.

That final theory sounds the most likely to me, but it doesn't hold any water when his brother, Sam, mysteriously reappears.

Sam survived against all odds and spent fifteen years incarcerated under terrible conditions, spending every long day wondering when his brother would come looking for him. His cellmate for the last two years was a powerful drug lord named Hector Alcazar, who was very interested in Sam's extensive knowledge of Henry Avery. Alcazar offered Sam his freedom in exchange for half of Avery's treasure, and if he failed to find it, Alcazar would kill him. Sam agreed, and Alcazar's cartel militia launched a full-scale attack on the guardhouse to break them out. After the prison break, Sam found Nathan as quickly as he could and asked for his help.

This reunion had to be powerfully bittersweet and confusing for Nate. Finding the treasure means he can finally close the chapter on losing his mom, and Sam's being alive means their dream of discovering it together isn't dead. But going with Sam means becoming the bloodthirsty man he used to be and breaking the trust of his wife. At the same time, keeping his promise to Elena means abandoning his poor brother again. The entire time Sam was in prison, Nathan was off galivanting in new, exotic places, charming beautiful women, and becoming a treasure-hunting legend. How incredibly guilty must he feel for abandoning Sam? How is he supposed to choose? It's an impossible problem he cannot run away from. And people he cares about are going to get hurt no matter what.

Of course Sam was able to persuade Nathan to help him, even if it meant breaking his promise with Elena. I mean, the game wouldn't be a game at all if Naughty Dog allowed the player to *not* follow this path. When it comes to a game like *Uncharted*, player choice is mainly relegated to action, not conflict. You choose how to approach a problem, but the game directs you to the story moments with the most impact by pushing Nathan further into the vise and forcing him to make the most conflicted decisions.

Nathan lies to Elena and joins his brother on the quest to find Avery's gold. He tells her he's going after an illegal salvage job in Malaysia, and she understands, knowing that he needs a bit of adventure in his life. But as a player, we can feel and see how this affects Nathan. He's short with his brother as the mission begins, and the snappy, witty dialogue we've always enjoyed with our main character is missing. Don't worry; it will return. This is Nathan Drake we're talking about, after all.

Uncharted 4: A Thief's End © Naughty Dog / Sony Computer Entertainment

It's this conflict between Nathan, Elena, and Sam that makes the next twenty plus hours of this game so darned compelling. The technique that the Naughty Dog writers use here is called layering. The earlier *Uncharted* stories had action-heavy plots filled with witty dialogue and clever puzzles. But *Uncharted 4* adds in a strong external conflict with very personal stakes—a villain promising to kill Nathan's brother. And then Naughty Dog goes the extra mile by adding internal conflict for Nathan to deal with—the guilt of leaving his brother behind and the decision to break his promise to his wife. On top of that, we have the context of hours and hours spent with Nathan in previous games all illuminated by the new understanding of his past and the potential deeper motivations for his choices. That's fantastic, deeply layered, complex storytelling.

We, as players, can't help but watch how the story unfolds, perhaps even bingeing all day and late into the night, because we must know how Nathan gets himself out of this situation. Our brains crave resolution. And the most satisfying resolution comes from well-designed internal character conflict.

Another technique Naughty Dog uses to really emphasize their point is narrative parallels. There are constant examples along the way to warn Nathan of his fate if he continues his path.

The first, most obvious example is that of the English pirate Henry Avery, captain of the *Fancy*. Avery, whose treasure the Drake brothers have always longed for, gained worldwide renown from orchestrating the largest heist of the 1600s, and he cemented his reputation as a clever tactician after uniting the world's most infamous pirates under one banner to form Libertalia, an island utopia, all under the guise of pursuing freedom from oppressive governments. Avery was gathering the criminal underground in one place to make it easier to steal their plunder for himself. He and his companion, Thomas Tew, poisoned the other founders and nearly made off with their riches until greed and paranoia consumed them and the two pirate captains killed each other in a final duel.

Greed in its purest form is responsible for Avery's descent into madness and ultimate demise; not even all the world's riches were enough to satisfy his hunger. Avery is the epitome of greed, and greed will consume until it eventually eats itself. Just like Henry Avery, Nathan is "a man of fortune, and [he] must seek [his] fortune." Nathan wants to find treasure despite his vow to Elena, and we can see he's not entirely satisfied with his life. Throughout the series, Nathan has been shown to have a singular inclination to find buried pirate treasure, and he breaks whatever rules or laws necessary to do so. The developers have shown us Nathan's flaws of greed and selfishness, and we, the players, are left to worry that he will make the same mistakes Avery did.

The second warning for Nathan Drake is told through a series of old, yellowed journal entries written by Jonathan Burnes, a distant relative to a member of Captain Avery's crew. Burnes left his wife, Claire, to search for the treasure, and in his eyes, any wrongdoing was justified because of the significant historical value and wealth the treasure held. In his final journal entry, he wrote, "In the end, I will have lived a life worth living. And Claire will be proud of me at long last. Claire. Forgive me."

This seemingly small parallel narrative highlights Nathan's selfishness, because he did the same thing to Elena. When he left, he could have died, going the way of Jonathan Burnes, and she wouldn't have known.

One final, less extreme but perhaps most relevant, warning to Nathan is the story of Evelyn. Evelyn was a world-renowned historian, famously pictured in exploration magazines beside once-great civilizations lost to time. During one of the flashbacks mentioned earlier, an eleven-year-old Nathan and his older brother, Sam, break into her estate to search for their mother's journals.

Evelyn's eerily silent house is filled to the brim with ancient artifacts, and the envious and obviously educated boys name the origin of time and place of each relic as they search through her home. There is an invitation addressed to Evelyn to attend an esteemed, exclusive explorers conference, and letters from admirers wishing to be as successful as she. This is a significant moment in the boys' lives. Everything important they once had—a family and a place to call home—is gone. Because they come from nothing, they have a strong desire to accomplish great things.

But they should not aspire to match Evelyn's degree of commitment to her occupation. She separated from her husband after the birth of their son, Edmund, in search of greater fortune. The stately home is adorned with valuables, but no one is inside to enjoy them. Evelyn's home is a lonely pile of gold in a dragon's den.

Inside a locked room next to a hospital bed surrounded by expensive-looking equipment and medical instruments, Nathan picks up a letter. Evelyn, in her rapidly deteriorating state, had been trying desperately to reconnect with her estranged son and grandchildren, but in the letter, Edmund asks her to leave him and his family alone for good. The last straw for him was when Evelyn did not attend her husband's funeral, a man who always loved and was patient with her even when she left them.

Evelyn spent her life filling her home with treasures, but in the end, the only true thing that could comfort her when she was alone was her family. A comfort she chose to forgo long ago, estranging those closest to her because of her ambition.

Captain Henry Avery, Jonathan Burnes, and Evelyn all believed that true happiness is found in fortune rather than family. These stories are all parallel narratives to Nathan and Sam's dogged attempts to find the treasure at any cost. They are warnings of what could happen to them if they continue down their path of indulgence.

Unfortunately, it seems as though the brothers are bent on repeating their mistakes. As the game progresses, we play along with Nathan as he devolves back into the single-minded treasure hunter from before. He begins to joke and play with Sam as they get closer to Avery's treasure. Many moments throughout this period of the story remind us of why we fell for Nathan in the first place. He has no fear, can climb anything, and knows more about the history and lore surrounding Avery than any person alive, and he's just a good brother. A good guy, even.

The interesting thing here is the protagonist doesn't redeem himself. Nathan didn't deserve to be rescued by Elena again. He chose to abandon her, twice. It's through the grace of the people who love him that he's redeemed. Elena's belief in Nathan's ability to overcome his selfishness is what redeems him. Without her there, Nathan would probably have died, and Rafe would have killed Sam. In this story, the damsel saves the hero in distress.

Unfortunately, Nathan follows his greedy desires, spiraling further away from the happy life he was working on before Sam returned. Sam takes things even further. He's so determined to find Avery's treasure that he betrays his own brother. In the years since the brothers separated, Nathan has grown. Sure, he's a thrill-seeking treasure hunter, but he has built meaningful relationships, carved out a life for himself, and generally found at least some balance in his life. Sam, not so much.

Sam becomes Nathan's foil. A foil is a character used to show us the motivations of one character in contrast to those of another. In this case, Sam is an example of what Nathan would have become if he hadn't experienced the growth that we've seen Nathan go through in the last three and a half games. Sam is emotionally stunted, vengeful, and very single-minded and selfish. He is willing to put his brother's life in grave danger, all for his personal gain.

Then there's Elena, who is the opposite of Sam. She's willing to do anything to save the man she loves. She is patient, kind, and generous. On the surface, she chases after Nathan to confront him about the lies and betrayal, but deeper down she does this because she cares about him. She cares about the two of them together. But she is also willing to let him make his mistakes, because she knows Nathan learns that way.

Uncharted 4: A Thief's End © Naughty Dog / Sony Computer Entertainment

These two characters, Sam and Elena, vengeance and grace, help round out Nathan as he sees both the good and bad inside these two important people in his life. It is through them that we see the fullness in Nathan's character.

In the end, the reason Nathan searches for treasure changes. And character change, growth, and learning are some of the reasons we love stories so much. He and Sam believed finding the treasure of Captain Avery would give them back what they lost when their mom died, but it wasn't true. It sounds cliché, but most true things are. Nathan realizes that all along the real treasure has been the people he loves.

In the final scene, you play several years into the future as Cassie Drake, Nathan and Elena's daughter. She walks through the house looking for her parents, but they aren't there. The Drakes are still an adventuring family; Sully and Sam take on more jobs together. She checks in Nate's office and finds his keys on the desk. She gets excited and unlocks a cabinet she obviously isn't allowed to look in. It's filled with treasures and memorabilia from the other *Uncharted* games. Elena and Nate catch her snooping, and Nate gets a little upset with her and embarrassed at what she found. In that moment, they decide it's appropriate to tell Cassie the stories of Nathan's previous life.

This happy ending is a direct juxtaposition to Evelyn's house, which was full of treasures but no one inside to enjoy them. Nathan's long-term change is expressed when he hides his treasure in a tiny closet he doesn't even want his daughter to learn about.

Uncharted 4 shows us that we all have the ability to change and that sometimes we just need someone to believe in us to give us the strength to do so. Elena believes Nathan can change and makes sacrifices for him time and time again despite his untrustworthiness. Nathan truly doesn't deserve her. But he does change despite himself, and thanks to the grace of Elena Drake.

Naughty Dog teaches a storytelling clinic with *Uncharted 4: A Thief's End*, by layering history, the present, and the future into a single nonlinear time line. The external and internal conflict play off each other like a complicated dance, until we are so invested in the story that we build an emotional connection with not just Nathan, but with all the main characters in this complex tale. But we can't forget, nor should we, how the blending of narrative and gameplay pull on two desires that we all share. The desire to learn from past mistakes, to tell and share great stories, and to be the best with one another in hopes of building a better tomorrow. To achieve our goals and best our foes, even if at times the most difficult enemy is ourselves.

BOOK REPORT:

Alan Wake

Alan Wake © Remedy

INITIAL RELEASE DATE AND PLATFORM:

May 2010 for Xbox 360 and Windows

WHERE ELSE CAN IT BE FOUND?

This game can be found on Steam for PC, and updated digital versions can be found for the Xbox One.

CATEGORY:

Nonlinear Narrative, Action/Adventure

MAIN CHARACTERS:

Alan Wake, a bestselling American author suffering from a two-year strain of writer's block

Alice Wake, Alan's wife

Barry, Alan's helpful friend

The Dark Presence, an environmental force beneath Cauldron Lake that has the power to turn fiction into reality

Barbara Jagger, an old woman who becomes the physical vessel for the Dark Presence

SETTING:

This story takes place in the Northwest corner of America, in the fictional community of Bright Falls. However, as the story moves along, alternate versions of reality take the player on a trippy adventure that is far more terrifying than the serene lakes and deep forests of Washington State.

Alan Wake © Remedy

Story Summary:

The night before Alan and his wife leave for a vacation to the mountain retreat in Bright Falls, Washington, Alan is haunted by a nightmare about shadowy figures trying to kill him.

When they arrive, a strange woman, the caretaker of the cabin they have rented, directs them to an island in the middle of Cauldron Lake. As they settle in, Alice and Alan argue, and Alan storms out of the cabin, only to be pulled back by his wife screaming for help.

What starts off as a story rooted in gritty realism turns paranormal as Alice is pulled into Cauldron Lake by a mysterious force.

The mystery only continues to grow as Alan and a helpful friend named Barry attempt to find Alice and unwind the oddities of Cauldron Lake. They discover the beginnings of a novel, called *Departure*, that Alan apparently wrote, although he has no recollection of doing so.

Will Alan be able to find Alice again? How is his writing involved in the solution? And what is up with this strange cabin in the first place? Well, you'll have to play it to find out, but I promise it will be worth it.

What Did You Think of This Story?

With the help of Barry, Alan is able to crack the mystery and discover how to rescue his wife, but it will be Alan alone who must take the steps to become the hero of his own story. This game goes on to throw surprise after surprise, always subverting the player's expectations and keeping them guessing. Alan needs to face his biggest fears, and as he does, they manifest in his reality, causing him to question his own sanity as the tension in the story goes from tight to unbearable.

I'd be lying if I said that the character's being a writer didn't have an effect on me. I've felt the discomfort of being creatively barren, and Alan's struggles with writer's block felt real and deeply explored. There's a nice metaphor between losing one's muse and Alan's losing his wife, and it continues as Alan is forced to fight through seemingly impossible odds and enemies to get her back. It's a gritty and oddly familiar story, while still providing excellent gameplay that kept me on the edge of my seat. I freaking loved this game, and I would suggest it to just about anyone with two big thumbs-up.

Storytelling Categories

What you enjoy reading, watching, or playing depends entirely on your tastes. It is totally valid to dislike something that is universally popular for no other reason than: "I just didn't like it." Let's say, hypothetically speaking, the popular thing you don't like is the *Super Mario Bros.* games. For whatever reason, they don't click with you. Maybe Mario's mustache offends you. Maybe you're disturbed by turtle violence. No matter what it is, you are entitled to your opinion.

HOWEVER, IF YOU WANT TO DISCUSS WHY YOU don't like *Super Mario Bros.*, relying solely on your preferences won't get you very far. Just because you don't like the game does not mean that it isn't well made and that everyone who likes it are a bunch of fools. It also doesn't mean you are a fool for not liking the athletic plumber, either.

Imagine, if you will, you are in court prosecuting the *Super Mario Bros.* video games. It is your responsibility to present a case explaining why the *Super Mario Bros.* games are inferior creations. If you have no evidence to support your claim, then your argument is going to fall flat and you'll lose favor with the judge and jury. You need to make your criticisms defensible by pointing out objective qualities about *Super Mario Bros.* that even someone who disagrees with you can relate to. When you combine well-researched structure with an impassioned speech about your subjective beliefs, that is when you have a moving argument.

Another example: I have been infatuated with the *Uncharted* franchise since Day One. But my fandom credentials are not enough of a reason to put the game in this book. I had to look past my feelings and point out specific, fair elements of the story to support my review. My arguments are nowhere near perfect, but I did spend countless hours playing and studying these games and have a load of experience working in story and games that I believe lends value to my voice as a critic.

What can really help is to define terms we can all agree on so that we're all speaking the same language. My hope is that most of you reading this are gamers and are familiar with phrases like online multiplayer or open-world third-person shooter. But, even if you're cozy with the game terms, you might not know as much about what theme is or what internal conflict is. Let alone something as unfamiliar as Freytag's Pyramid.

It can feel daunting to newcomers when faced with new words, terms, and phrases. For example, Twitch, the popular video game streaming website, is like a distant alien planet to me. It has a culture and vocabulary all its own that I have not even begun to translate.

While we can recognize good stories and have preferences about which stories we consider great, not everyone can inherently tell a good story off the top of their head. If that were the case, we would all enjoy year-round vacations from our bestselling books and billion-dollar video game franchises. There are actual hard skills writers can develop to improve their craft, and studying great stories is one of those exercises.

That is why it's especially important when critiquing something to build a common understanding of terms. It helps to have a library of recognized literary devices, storytelling and gameplay genres, to ground your feelings and to learn how the creators of the games you love use them to build stories with impact.

With that said, since this is a book that assesses storytelling in video games, let's go back and reestablish a definition for what a story is.

I stated at the opening of this book that a story is when a character faces an unavoidable, challenging obstacle, and how they change because of it. It is an account of events or incidents, or the plot of a dramatic or narrative work. And while I stand by those definitions, it's okay to dig in a bit and talk about how that applies in games.

And while we're at it, let's take a crack at defining different types of storytelling you might find in games. There are three major camps of narrative styles: linear, nonlinear, and what I am going to call branching narrative.

A linear narrative begins at point A and connects through checkpoints in sequential order until point Z, where the story ends. *The Last of Us* (part 1, not 2), *Brothers*, *God of War*, *Portal*, and many more games fit into this category. Actually, movies, aside from very few outliers, fit in this category as well. You hit Play, the story moves forward, you eat popcorn until the credits roll, and the lights come on.

A nonlinear narrative is when events are experienced out of order when time line is concerned. In this instance, the story might start at H, then go back to C, then skip ahead to I, J, and K, before going back to A. Eventually, the story will stitch together as we learn important events that happened in the life of our characters until we arrive at the resolution and the story wraps up at Z once again. It's a mixed-up alphabet, but in the end all the letters are still represented.

It's often shown to us in flashbacks, distinctive plotlines outside the main story, or parallel narratives. We might read about a character's background after spending some time with them in the present. Then we might skip ahead twenty years to see how their decisions could affect the story. A well-known example of this is Charles Dickens's *A Christmas Carol*, where, in the span of a single night, we see the past, present, and future of Ebenezer Scrooge, allowing us to see how he became the man he is now, and how the world might change if he is unwilling to change himself.

Uncharted, which we just covered in some depth, uses this device as well. *Halo 3: ODST*, *Metal Gear Solid 4*, and *Batman: Arkham Asylum* are also great examples of this mechanic.

Finally, the least common style, branching narrative, makes the player feel as though they have the power to change the story. In this style, the story still starts at Point A, but there might be two point Bs to choose from, and three or four point Cs. And which ones you choose might affect which points D, E, and F are available. And in some extreme cases, the ending might not be Z. It might be W, X, Y, or Z.

Any story that offers the player a choice to significantly change the plot is a branching narrative. There are very few examples of branching storytelling in literature, but one of the things I find most appealing about video games is their capacity to use this style more effectively. Branching narratives often have multiple endings, as you can see in games like *NieR: Automata*, *Detroit: Become Human*, and *Undertale*.

What sets these stories apart from something like *Uncharted 4*, for instance, which is a nonlinear narrative, is that in *Uncharted*, the player does not have power over any of the major plot points in the story (they can't choose whether Nathan lies to Elena, for example). And *Uncharted* has only one ending, which every player experiences the same way.

It's also possible to have a nonlinear branching style. *The Witcher 3*, for example, includes flashbacks and other events that take place out of the current time line, but it also has a narrative that changes depending on the player's choices.

Regardless of the mechanic or literary device used to craft a story, it is important to remember that characters show change. They are not the same person at the end of the tale that they were when the story began. When it comes to story, change is king.

BOOK REPORT:

Silent Hill 2

Silent Hill 2 © Konami

INITIAL RELEASE DATE AND PLATFORM:

September 2001 for PlayStation 2

WHERE ELSE CAN IT BE FOUND?

After the initial launch, the game was rereleased on the Xbox, PlayStation 3, Xbox 360, and Windows PC. Finding a modern version might be tough, but if you can get your hands on the original PS2 version, it will totally be worth it.

Category:

Branching Narrative, Horror

Main Characters:

James Sunderland, the main (playable) character

Mary Sunderland, James's deceased wife

Maria, arguably the primary antagonist of *Silent Hill 2*. She also looks identical to Mary.

Eddie Dombrowski, a sad character, who has turned a life of being bullied into one of rage-filled, drunken violence

Angela Orosco, a young woman with a traumatic past who is searching the town for her missing mother

Laura, a young girl and the symbol of youth and innocence in the game

Pyramid Head, a humanoid monster whose head is completely obscured by a giant, metal, pyramid-shaped helmet

Setting:

The game is named after the city you play in, Silent Hill, Maine. Most of the game is played in the nightmarish illusions the city creates (Otherworld) for those who have traveled there. Full of fog, strange buildings, and darkness, it is the perfect setting for this haunting tale.

Story Summary:

James, who lost his wife three years prior, has received a note from her, written in her handwriting, asking him to meet her in their favorite place. James knows exactly where that is. Curious and energized, he hops into his car and zips to the town of Silent Hill.

Once there, James is forced to confront the reality of his

poor decision-making as he visits with four very disturbed, or disturbing, characters: Eddie, a violent, simple drunk who sees the town filled with bullies of his past who have teased and taunted him. Angela, an attractive, compelling woman, who sees and experiences fire everywhere. Laura, a six-year-old girl who seems to walk through Silent Hill unaffected by the horrible monsters that haunt the town. And Maria, a woman who looks exactly like James's dead wife, who is forced, in the game, to die over and over as James watches helplessly.

Just who is Maria, and what happened to Mary, James's wife? And why is he forced to witness her death over and over again as he struggles to battle the terrifying demons around him?

WHAT DID YOU THINK OF THIS STORY?

The entire Silent Hill franchise is a trippy stumble down a horror-filled alley. In their own right, each of the games could be mentioned, but *Silent Hill 2* is particularly strange and wonderful in all the right ways. When it first came out on the PlayStation 2 in 2001, it set a standard for playing with the power of the gaming medium by offering a bizarre, nightmare-fueled experience that made the player question reality as they joined James, the protagonist, on his quest to find his wife.

Or at least, that's what the game wants us to believe.

This game is twenty years old, and it has aged to perfection. While the visuals and some of the gameplay itself have been replaced by the higher fidelity offered by today's powerhouse consoles, the story and mystery found in *Silent Hill 2* is as innovative today as it was when it was created. Packed with symbolism and metaphor, we learn that perhaps nothing in the world is real at all and that certainly everyone who visits the town sees it in their own way. Compelling character revelations push this story forward and keep you guessing until the very end.

Best played in the dark with a loud sound system, this branching narrative game with multiple endings will not only make you worry about what lurks around the corner, but it will also make you more and more angry at James as you learn who the true monster of Silent Hill is. This masterpiece is a must play for any horror-loving story addict.

Persona 5

Metaphor (N.)

A metaphor compares two similar things by saying that one of them *is* the other. A figure of speech in which a term or phrase is applied to something to which it is literally applicable in order to suggest a resemblance. For example, "He was a monster."

PERSONA 5 IS A NONLINEAR BRANCHING NARRA-tive, villain-of-the-week style JRPG game about teens rebelling against unfair authority, symbolized as actual prisons, and fighting to break free by confronting your true, furious nature. The game is packed with angst and charged with a unique visual flair that gives a stylish mood and atmosphere to one of the most memorable visual works of metaphor in modern literature. Every inch of this game oozes creativity. If you've played it before, you're probably hearing the jazzy, kinetic soundtrack in your head right now. Sound over the top? Dive into this game and after a few minutes you'll know exactly what I mean.

Persona 5 © *Atlus*

The *Persona* series as a whole is inspired by the theories of psychologist Carl Jung, who famously proposed that everyone wears a persona, a kind of mask intended to conform to group norms and conceal the true self and could be classified into common archetypes that determined one's superficial personality. In *Persona 5*, each character takes on a unique archetype, like the fool, the magician, and the lover. However, the writers don't just leave us with these two-dimensional character sketches, they round them out with more depth to make each character complex and interesting.

There are over a dozen character archetypes in *Persona 5*, and to keep the story focused, each character's journey centers on a singular theme, which tells us the only way they can live free is by recognizing the abusive powers they have condoned to rule over their lives and choosing to listen to their rebellious wills and bite back.

You, as the player, get to decide the name of the story's protagonist, but regardless of what you choose, the other characters in the world will refer to him by his nickname, Joker. You never actually learn the true name of the protagonist. Part of the reason for that is to make the player feel as though they are Joker, taking part in the story.

Joker from Persona 5 © Atlus

While Joker is the star of the story, almost every major character you meet has an individual arc surrounding a subtheme represented by a tarot card. This is another connection to Jung, who likened archetypes to a tarot deck and believed you could look beyond someone's persona and learn about their true self by studying tarot readings. Chihaya Mifune, for example, tells fortunes with tarot cards and uses her cheerful disposition to mask a dark past. Futaba Sakura is the hermit arcana, a shut-in who learns to accept herself and not let her past define her. And Tae Takemi is the death arcana, who had a spiritual death when her career as a promising physician was unjustly terminated and has to change her philosophy about what it means to be a healer. The symbolism of the tarot cards provides us with a shortcut to understanding the characters' conflicts by tapping into their core natures. While they don't add a load of depth to the characters themselves, they round out the universe and give us context that helps us attach to the massive cast.

These three tiny character breakdowns are only a small sample of the ten extensive story lines you can experience in this tour de force of storytelling content. There's no way I can cover everything in this epic yarn. It's so massive we really only have time to cover one boss and a couple of the main characters, but the overall thrust of the remainder of the game is equal in every aspect. It's a compelling, awesome body of work, which can take a player on a multi-hundred-hour journey of discovery. I'm serious. Multi. Hundred. Hours.

Joker himself portrays the Joker tarot card. No secrets there. The Joker in the deck traditionally represents zero. A character that includes all and nothing, seriousness and jokes, happiness and sorrow. A perfect character for us, as the player, to replace in the story emotionally.

Joker's story begins late one night, when he rushes to the aid of a woman in distress. She is being assaulted by an intoxicated man wearing dark glasses and a suit. She cries for help as he reaches for her, but Joker pushes the man out of the way. The man stumbles to the ground and threatens to sue the youth. He calls over a nearby officer and accuses Joker of assaulting him before being helped into a limousine. Every element of this moment is designed intentionally, from the tailored suit to the shades he hides behind as he stumbles drunkenly into his expensive car. They are all symbols of wealth and power. The police take the older gentleman's word over that of the suspicious teen and arrest Joker. He is subsequently expelled from school, and his parents, disappointed and ashamed, send him away to live in the attic of a coffee shop owned by a strict man named Sojiro Sakura. There, Joker is ordered to attend Shujin Academy to be rehabilitated.

This opening scene of discrimination propels the story forward and promises Joker's life will never be the same. In literary terms, this is called the inciting incident, a moment in time that changes the trajectory of the main character.

Not long afterward, Joker dreams of being imprisoned in a place called the Velvet Room. There, we learn that his first action of standing up to the rich man, and the resulting unfair punishment by forces abusing their power, has drawn the attention of powerful beings from something called the Metaverse. These beings recognize his rebellious spirit and strong sense of justice, and they have chosen him as their hero to fight against greater injustice in the world. This prison motif is something the game will return to again and again as scores of innocent people are taken advantage of by the privileged.

Before Joker leaves for the first day at his school, his caretaker, Sakura-san, reminds him to keep his nose clean and stay out of trouble. Even the game's quest menus tell Joker to obey the rules: Don't miss curfew, make it to school on time, go to class. While Joker is on the subway, he notices a strange red-and-black app with a stylized eye pop up on his phone that he can't delete. Televisions on the subway broadcast news reports of unexplained mishaps in Tokyo, mass hysteria and memory loss, a bus crash in Shujin, and a particularly disastrous event involving the deaths of dozens in a runaway train. As Joker reaches his station and walks through the city, he overhears conversations of people who are worried about the direction the country is headed. They fear economic collapse and corruption in the police force and among politicians, and they are concerned about the growing number of tragedies.

Within walking distance of the academy, Joker meets a girl named Ann Takamaki, one of the story's main characters. She offers Joker a pleasant smile, then a car pulls up in front of the two and the window rolls down. The arrogant-looking man behind the wheel is wearing a matching blue jumper and sweatpants with a white stripe down the side. He offers Ann a ride, and her expression falls. She unwillingly accepts and stares at her hands as she slips into the passenger seat. The man introduces himself to Joker as Suguru Kamoshida, former Olympic gold medalist and head coach of the prestigious Shujin volleyball team. He is about to offer Joker a ride, but the car speeds off as Ryuji Sakamoto, another main character, sprints up from behind Joker, saying something derisive after Kamoshida. Something about his being a pervert.

This rush of characters and a world already in shambles might seem like a lot to take in all at once. And believe me, that is deliberate. It's chaotic and is meant to show how it feels to be placed in an unfamiliar universe, where everything around you is changing. Anyone who has experienced entering a new school, whether it's shifting from middle school to high school, or by moving to a new location, can feel the tension and anxiety bubbling up in Joker. It's well done, and when we meet Ryuji, his offer to slow things down and just talk for a bit is a welcome change of pace.

Ryuji introduces himself and is surprised to find that Joker is the new transfer student. The criminal. Somehow, rumors of his arrest had traveled to the students at the school. Ryuji is a troublemaker, too, and doesn't act intimidated by Joker's already infamous reputation. Ryuji offers to show him the way to school, but they need to get moving. It wouldn't look good if the two students with the worst reputations showed up late together on their first day.

But that is where things take a turn for the weird. On their way to Shujin Academy, the world takes on a strange purple tint, and instead of the school, they find a gigantic medieval castle rising from the mist. Bemused by the strange turn of events, Ryuji and Joker walk to the gate and knock to see if anyone is inside. To their surprise, knights in gleaming armor capture them and throw them into a dark dungeon. Moments later, Kamoshida, the volleyball coach from earlier, menacingly parades in front of the thick iron bars of their prison. But there is something off about him. Not only has he swapped out his tracksuit for an ornate velvet cape covered in red hearts, a crown, and a pink Speedo, but his eyes are bright yellow and he's unabashedly evil. Like a stereotypical cartoon villain, cheesy monologues and all.

Persona 5 is doing something special here, using symbolism and metaphor in a very literal way. It allows the gamer to play through these metaphorical stages and set pieces. Not only do Joker and Ryuji feel trapped by their lives, but now they actually are trapped in a dungeon cell.

In the fictional world of *Persona 5*, there are two realms: the physical and the cognitive. Both realms live on top of each other, but in different dimensions, and only people with special capabilities can travel to and from the cognitive realm, called the Metaverse. The physical realm is similar to the reality we live in today, while the invisible Metaverse is a mirror that reflects the emotions, or personas, of people in the physical realm in relevant, exaggerated ways. The more distorted, or wicked, the person is in the physical realm, the more powerful their shadow in the cognitive. These shadows are literal metaphors. The people who act like monsters in the physical realm become actual monsters in the Metaverse. *Persona*

5 doesn't just *tell* us these two realms are inseparable, it *shows* us by linking them together thematically throughout the game.

We've seen what Kamoshida looks like in the physical realm, and we get a little taste of his personality, a hint that something is wrong when he invites Ann into his car. Her obviously downcast body language telegraphs the fact that she had no other choice but to accept. Now, in the Metaverse, Joker and Ryuji can see behind Kamoshida's mask and find themselves in the clutches of his shadow, or true self. Kamoshida is a monster.

Ryuji, who has a painful history with the evil volleyball coach, spits an insult at him and demands to be released. Shadow Kamoshida sentences the teens to death for offending the king. Scared and confused, the boys can't tell if they are talking to the real Kamoshida or if it's all just a horrible nightmare. The guards chain Joker to the wall, where he is forced to watch helplessly as Kamoshida beats Ryuji to a pulp. If it's a dream, then it is awfully convincing.

What makes the Metaverse such a dramatic storytelling device is that simply *seeing* Shadow Kamoshida is more than enough to communicate what the real Kamoshida thinks of himself; that he is a king, the school is his castle, and any dissidents who don't toe the line or who wound his fragile ego must be put to death.

To intensify the nightmarish feeling, the corners of Joker's mind are filled with an ominous, disembodied voice. It challenges Joker's motivations, asking if he is truly fighting for Ryuji's life or if he is fighting to save his own skin. The voice questions whether Joker meant it when he stood up for the woman in the street or if it was a fluke. To prove himself, Joker strains against his chains and shouts at Kamoshida to stop. Surprised, the villain drops a coughing and sputtering Ryuji to the dusty stone floor. He turns around to kill

Joker instead, but a rushing pulse emanates from Joker through the dingy chamber, freezing time for everyone but Joker. When he awakes and lifts up his head, there is a mask stuck to his face. Screaming, he rips it off in a shower of blood, and it is replaced by a mask of blue fire. The ominous voice laughs wickedly from the inferno and transforms into a demon with black feathery wings and a red suit. Its powerful wings spectacularly break the chains that surrounded Joker, and he boldly introduces himself as Arsene, the pillager of twilight.

When Joker tears off the mask, a symbol of the personality archetype he puts on to be accepted by society, he accepts his true nature to rebel against corruption. Arsene is his shadow persona in the Metaverse, a representation of his defiant spirit. Before Arsene will help him, he makes Joker promise to fight against tyranny whenever he sees it.

Some of the guards scramble out of the cell in fear, and Kamoshida, cowering, orders those that remain to kill Arsene and Joker. The turn-based combat starts as Joker commands Arsene to use his otherworldly powers to defeat the guards and rescue Ryuji. They escape the cell, but not before locking Kamoshida in behind them. Arsene disappears as the confused pair run through the dungeon seeking an exit, away from the echoing shouts of their gym teacher.

Joker and Ryuji run past cells filled with high school students in volleyball uniforms sporting bruises and casts, symbolizing Kamoshida's abuse of his players. They try to help, but the students don't want to be rescued.

Just when Joker and Ryuji thought things couldn't get any stranger, they find an inmate completely different from the others:

a talking cat. He introduces himself as Morgana, and he promises to show them the way out if they help him. The two free Morgana, and he explains that he is a human trapped inside a cat's body, another metaphor for imprisonment. Morgana becomes your guide to the Metaverse and helps teach the player about combat and other mechanics as the game progresses.

The talking cat leads them outside to the front gates, and they part ways. Ryuji and Joker were stuck in the castle for what felt like hours, and unfortunately for them, upon returning to the real world, it appears that time moves at the same speed in the cognitive realm, and the two are late to class on the first day, confirming their reputations as troublemakers.

Persona 5 © Atlus

Throughout the days, Joker is treated by his new teachers as if he were a dangerous criminal and could snap at any minute. Even Joker's caretaker, Sakura-san the coffee shop owner, is just waiting for Joker to do something violent. But despite the treatment Joker receives from everyone around him, he still feels he did the right thing by standing up for that woman. And he's proud that he stood up for Ryuji, too. Sharing a similar near-death experience and being treated like crooks with no future forge a bond between the two young men from the very start. For better or worse, he and Ryuji become as thick as thieves.

We soon learn that Ryuji is very motivated to get vengeance on Kamoshida, and for good reason. About a year ago, Ryuji was the star of the track team but was resented by Kamoshida, who was the assistant coach at the time. Kamoshida wanted to push his athletes to dangerous levels beyond their limits, and Ryuji was the only one who stood up to him. Kamoshida purposefully provoked Ryuji by spreading rumors to the team about his father, who drunkenly beat Ryuji and left his mom. Ryuji couldn't take the harassment any longer and one day exploded in outrage and punched Kamoshida. In response, and using the excuse of self-defense, Kamoshida broke the teenager's leg, bringing his running career to a swift end. The resulting skirmish totally dismantled the track team, and Kamoshida made sure that he came out looking like the victim and that Ryuji looked like the person who ruined everything. Kamoshida was rewarded by the system and promoted to head coach of the volleyball team, which he vaulted to national success because of his experience as an Olympic gold medalist. Kamoshida still holds Ryuji's assault over him, and even loosely threatens to break his other leg if he doesn't like the way Ryuji looks at him in the halls. The dude is so easy to hate, and that hatred only grows as we learn more about Ann Takamaki's story.

Ann is a model who Kamoshida has been blackmailing for certain favors by threatening to remove Shiho Suzui, Ann's best friend, from the starting lineup of the girls' volleyball team. Ann has been walking a fine line, trying to keep close enough to the coach without getting too serious in order to protect Shiho. One night, Kamoshida messages Ann, telling her to visit his house, but she declines. He tells her she is going to regret rejecting him, and the next day Shiho tries to commit suicide. Apparently, Kamoshida had been verbally and physically abusing Shiho, and the night Ann rejected him, he assaulted Shiho. Ann knew what happened to Shiho wasn't her fault, but she couldn't help but blame herself.

Joker, Ryuji, and Ann's backstories show us that *Persona 5* understands that a character's motivations need to be believable. Not only do they want to fight against Kamoshida because they have a general, objective sense of right and wrong, they also want to fight him because they have personal stakes in making sure Kamoshida pays for his cruelty. The writers for *Persona 5* knew that the true power of a story lies in making characters act based on practical, personal experiences that will affect them in the moment. The three are bound together by similar experiences, and they find greater camaraderie in seeking justice for others who also feel oppressed.

Over various trips to the Metaverse, both Ryuji and Ann unlock their own shadow personas and vow to take justice into their own hands. And Morgana has a plan for how they can accomplish that.

If they enter the Metaverse and defeat the Shadow Kamoshida, they can change the real Kamoshida's evil intentions. But it won't be easy. The only way to do it is to steal his heart. Hidden somewhere deep in Kamoshida's Metaverse palace is an object from the real world that embodies his distorted desires. If they can steal it, the real Kamoshida should lose his distorted desires and confess to his crimes on his own.

The teens commit to entering the castle and committing a large-scale heist, which has to be completed before the real Kamoshida has them expelled. They combine to form the Phantom Thieves, vigilante heroes who bend the rules to serve their own form of justice to wrongdoers, starting with Kamoshida.

As the evil Kamoshida has continued to find confidence in his devious ways in the physical realm, he has continued to grow in the cognitive world. After a long fight through Kamoshida's castle, the team finally makes it to the throne room, beyond which is the vault that holds his treasure, the source of his distorted desires. But first, they have to defeat Kamoshida himself, who has transformed into a gluttonous giant with a long purple tongue, four arms, and puffy eyes. The metaphors of this greedy man and his disgusting habits are on full display. Three of his grubby hands hold glittering, golden cutlery, and in the one he holds a wineglass filled with the upside-down legs of female mannequins. At his feet are volleyball slaves locked to the ground with golden ball-and-chain traps, and a championship trophy full of more mannequin legs.

The battle commences, and thanks to a diversion by one of the Phantom Thieves, they prove victorious. The giant Kamoshida deflates into the slimy coward he has always been, and as the team surrounds him, they allow Ann to make the final choice to deal with Kamoshida. She pauses before delivering a final, resounding blow. Although Ann is filled with rage, she decides that Kamoshida has no right to escape from his guilt and instead deserves to live with it and atone.

Kamoshida couldn't let go of his past glory of winning an Olympic medal. He couldn't accept that someone of his status, with such grand achievements, should teach high school brats. He used the

Ann, Ryuji, and Joker from Persona 5 © Atlus

opportunity at Shujin to force his insecurities onto his poor students. He took advantage of inexperienced young people with his position because they were easy for him to control, and he turned the academy into his personal den of iniquity. On the outside, he appeared to others as a handsome, accomplished athlete, but on the inside, he was just as repulsive as his Shadow.

The Phantom Thieves leave the squirming Shadow Kamoshida behind to find the treasure, the source of Kamoshida's distorted desires. Behind the throne, in his royal bedroom, on piles of gold, lies a giant crown. They swipe the prize and transport back to the physical realm, where the crown transforms into a replica of Kamoshida's Olympic gold medal, the physical manifestation of his distorted desires. Days later, Kamoshida holds an assembly and confesses his numerous crimes in front of the entire student body and tearfully begs for their forgiveness. He is arrested that same day.

By allowing us to experience both the cognitive and physical realms, *Persona 5* harnesses the power of metaphor to tell a difficult story. The Metaverse is a brilliant storytelling mechanic that is used to great effect. While *Persona 5* doesn't shy away from expository dialogue and villain monologues, it also shows us the internal lives of these villains, with amazingly elaborate set pieces to explore fantastic encounters and momentously striking visuals. And it's taken one step further by allowing the player to interact with the metaphorical representations of physical weakness and traits in the enemies in the game. *Persona 5* gives us the chance to make those metaphors feel literal. Sure, it's satisfying to beat the snot out of a goobery pile of greed in a video game, but when that monster is the actual, exaggerated manifestation of someone who uses his position of power to abuse vulnerable students, it is just so much more satisfying.

Remember when I mentioned this game was huge? Well, I wasn't lying. Kamoshida's story is only a sample of the many characters and conflicts you'll find in this epic game. At its simplest, it could be defined as a high school simulator, filled with mythological beasts and battles, but you and I know better. *Persona 5* is a deeply personal story, which appropriately tackles dark, sensitive topics while still feeling as though there is a light at the end of the tunnel. It gives you the power to fight against insurmountable odds in your own life, even if people around you think you shouldn't. It's an extraordinary piece of art, which made me feel the most punk rock I've felt in my entire life.

BOOK REPORT:

Grim Fandango

Grim Fandango © Lucasarts

INITIAL RELEASE DATE AND PLATFORM:

October 30, 1998, for Microsoft Windows and Classic Mac OS

Where Else Can It Be Found?

Well, the good news is that this game is not only easy to find, but the remastered version from 2015 looks and plays great. You can find it for Mac and PC on Steam today.

Category:

Linear Narrative, Story Game, with a dash of humor

Main Characters:

Manny Calavera, our protagonist, a travel agent for the Land of the Dead from the Department of Death

Mercedes "Meche" Colomar, a woman who lived a good life but is cheated out of her ticket to heaven

Domino Hurley, Manny's coworker, a corrupt agent who forges tickets to heaven for the boss of the criminal underworld

Hector LeMans, the boss of the afterlife's criminal underworld and all-around bad dude

Setting:

Grim Fandango takes place in the Land of the Dead (the Eighth Underworld), where recently departed souls aim to make their way to the Land of Eternal Rest (the Ninth Underworld) on the Four-Year Journey of the Soul.

Story Summary:

Manny Calavera is a travel agent for the Land of the Dead, a transitional place where souls go to make their journey to the next level of existence. If you've lived a good life, you get a golden ticket on the Number Nine train to heaven. If you led an evil life, all you get is a walking cane to prepare you for a four-year trek on foot across the land. Lately, his co-salesman, Domino, is getting all the golden-ticket passengers, while Manny is only getting evil souls. Manny hijacks the soul of Meche, a woman who has lived a good and pure life; but the system indicates that she was evil and must walk. Realizing that Domino is running a scam that changes how souls are sorted for eternity, Manny heads out on a four-year mission to stop this dastardly plot, save the soul of the beautiful Meche, and hopefully gain some redemption for himself in the process.

WHAT DID YOU THINK OF THIS STORY?

This game is delightful in every way. The dialogue is witty, the jokes really land, and the playful and inspired art style holds up today as well as it did when it was created. Not to mention *Grim Fandango* was one of the first games where we got to see Tim Schafer really flex his game-writing muscles. The tone of this game is as unique as it comes.

Adding humor to a video game is a dangerous endeavor. Jokes fall flat more often than not. But *Grim Fandango* is a clinic on how to write humor into the world, as well as the dialogue. Schafer spins the three motifs of the Day of the Dead, hard-boiled detective film noir, and travel agencies into a bizarre and interesting mix that comes off as funny, clever, and memorable. For me, it isn't just the dialogue that is funny, but the game is set in such a fun world that I'm constantly delighted. It's packed with opportunities to keep me guessing. If I had two words to describe this game, I think I'd go with surprising and delightful.

Tim Schafer is an icon in the video game storytelling world, and the moment you're done checking this out, run and sample some of his other masterpieces, such as *Day of the Tentacle*, *Psychonauts*, and *The Secret of Monkey Island*.

Plot— Above-the- Neck Verbs Versus Below- the-Neck Verbs

Plot (N.)

Plot is a sequence of events in a story, where each affects the next, through a principle of cause and effect.

Plot Versus Gameplay

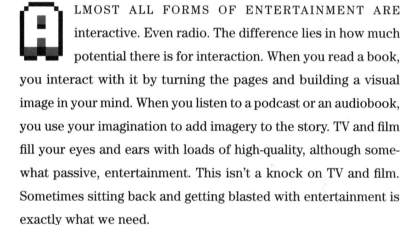

LMOST ALL FORMS OF ENTERTAINMENT ARE interactive. Even radio. The difference lies in how much potential there is for interaction. When you read a book, you interact with it by turning the pages and building a visual image in your mind. When you listen to a podcast or an audiobook, you use your imagination to add imagery to the story. TV and film fill your eyes and ears with loads of high-quality, although somewhat passive, entertainment. This isn't a knock on TV and film. Sometimes sitting back and getting blasted with entertainment is exactly what we need.

However, the potential for interactivity with video games is determined by the limits of human ingenuity. Compare these two games: *Zork* and *Guitar Hero*. *Zork* is an interactive fiction game from the late 1970s. Text is displayed on the screen to feed you the plot and action, and the player is asked to read, imagine, then type a text-based response to move things forward. Fast-forward a couple of decades later to *Guitar Hero*, and you play with a plastic guitar with six fret buttons and a strum bar. You live out your fantasy as a rock star on stage, performing classic rock hits to sold-out crowds screaming your name.

Because there is so much room for creative interactivity, it makes plot unique, and it slightly changes how it's defined in the context of video games.

I'll use *Super Mario Bros.* as an example of what I mean. The game industry's favorite hero/plumber runs through a colorful fantasy world, where he jumps/smashes turtles and mushrooms while platforming through a complex puzzle world full of hidden items, goodies, and power-ups. His world can be as simple as running and jumping at times, but then things get difficult. The game can turn into a pixel-perfect timing game that requires the player to press buttons at precise times to narrowly avoid everything from bouncing fireballs to bullets the size of washing machines. This weaving, jumping, ducking, smashing action is all external conflict. It's blood-pumping and addicting. A lot of games out there offer just this and nothing more, which isn't a bad thing. I like to think of this type of action as below-the-neck motivation. Running, jumping, shooting, fighting . . . you get the idea. The motivation is *physical*, and the character has to *act* to survive.

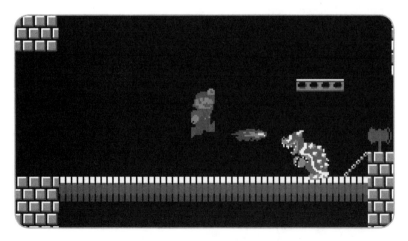

Super Mario Bros. © *Nintendo*

And this is where the separation between traditional storytelling mediums and video games comes into play. In a video game, below-the-neck verbs are usually what the player controls, the gameplay. Often when we talk about what makes a game fun, which is nearly impossible to define, these below-the-neck verbs are what we are talking about. If there is a difficulty setting, usually the things that are affected when you change them are below-the-neck verbs. Generally, the things that happen in the story that the player does not control, or does not change, is plot.

In *Super Mario Bros.*, the below-the-neck verbs, like run, duck, and jump, are gameplay-related. And the plot, albeit simple, of saving the princess is narrative-related, or narrative plot.

The point I'm getting at here is that video games don't need a story to be entertaining. Being highly interactive is enjoyable enough that you could go your whole life as a fan of video games and never play a single story-focused game. Would you ever turn the pages of a book without reading the story just for fun? I wouldn't judge you if you did, but come on. If you want something fun to do without a story, try out a video game like *Overwatch* or *Minecraft*. Those games are chock-full of below-the-neck motivation and are incredibly addicting. They may have elements that other narrative-driven games possess, like role-playing (power fantasy) as a character, but they are not storytelling video games by design. It's also worth pointing out that neither of these games contain plot. Sure, there's some *Minecraft* and *Overwatch* lore that lives on outside the game world, but in the games themselves, there is no plot to move the story forward.

INTERNAL CONFLICT, THE SECRET INGREDIENT

The gameplay of a story-based video game should be fun, but it is not the source of its true power. As gamers, we can confuse the story in a video game to be the fun mechanics. It may be fun to duck under an enemy's cover fire by ducking behind a trashed-out minivan, but ultimately, that stuff is, while fun, not there to drive a lot of depth. While you are experiencing a story, you are invariably seeking a few specific elements, whether you know it or not. And those things are the same across all platforms: books, movies, comics, video games, podcasts, you name it.

What generates a powerful story is when a protagonist is in a challenging situation, struggles with what matters most to them, and makes hard decisions that progress the narrative forward. A believable character lives true to the pains and fears caused by emotional hardships in their lives that keep them from their impossible goals. Story is not just about the plot, or what happens to them. It is when a character undergoes an internal change because of the plot impacts, and how that affects them.

All stories rely on this special ingredient, internal conflict, what the character thinks and feels about the things happening to them. I call these above-the-neck verbs. While below-the-neck verbs are related to a character's physical well-being, above-the-neck verbs relate to a character's emotional well-being, which is just as important to our survival. If not more so. Games without above-the-neck verbs to give meaning to the action are generally not storytelling video games. They have their place; some of my favorite video games are totally void of internal conflict, but they tend to lack emotional impact.

Above-the-neck verbs are the second half of the cause-and-effect principle—the things the character thinks, or feels, when the plot poses a problem they cannot avoid. For example, when Sam reappears in Nathan's life, it means Nate has to reconcile his emotions from his conflicted past and what he must do because of it. Along the way, Nathan makes grave mistakes regarding his closest personal relationships to hide his shame, but in the end, he learns that he should have been honest with them in the first place. Reconciliation, guilt, shame, confusion, sorrow, and joy. These above-the-neck verbs are what gives the action in a story purpose. Without them, the momentum is lost and the plot is stuck cold in its tracks.

We've all had stories affect us in meaningful ways. We passed down stories for millennia, warning of physical dangers and, perhaps more important, of sociological and psychological dangers to preserve the human race. As technology advanced, so did our techniques to use that technology to tell stories.

Stories aren't the only thing that forge deep, biological memories. Competition is an innate part of our biology as well. You've heard of survival of the fittest, right? Well, a big part of that is our ability, our drive, to compete. Games tap into this desire to best others, whether that is against nonplayable characters or directly with other human players in online games. We love to test our skills, prove that we are champions, and reap the rewards for our conquest.

There's something incredibly addicting for some and meaningful for others when we combine these two huge biological drivers: competition and story. It isn't new. Sports have tapped into this phenomenon for centuries. Politics? You bet. Video games are wholly unique because they take full advantage of letting the player experience the below-the-neck verbs of a story in a more tactile way than any other medium. And for me, how interactivity can potentially translate to make a story more compelling makes this art form significant historically.

BOOK REPORT:

NieR: Automata

NieR: Automata © PlatinumGames / Square Enix

INITIAL RELEASE DATE AND PLATFORM:

February 2017 for PlayStation 4, Xbox One, Windows PC

CATEGORY:

Branching Narrative, Action Role-Playing Game

Main Characters:

YoRHa No. 2 Type B (2B), an all-purpose battle android, deployed as a member of the automated YoRHa infantry. She is equipped with a multitude of weapons for close-quarters combat and can attack from a range using the Pod support system.

YoRHa No. 9 Type S (9S), a scanner type android who served during the Fourteenth Machine War. He has an attack function but specializes in investigative purposes.

Setting:

In the year AD 11945, invaders from another world and human-made androids find themselves locked into a proxy war. While most of the androids are nameless and emotionally cold, the protagonists have individuality and attributes that distinguish them from their fellow bots. The YoRHa android forces are commanded from the Bunker, a reconnaissance base in orbit above Earth. They fight alongside the pre-YoRHa androids on Earth (known as the Resistance) to drive back the Machines.

Story Summary:

Ten thousand years from now, humanity has evacuated the planet, abandoning Earth to the YoRHa androids created to fight a mysterious race of alien invaders and their army of Machines.

2B is one of the android warriors, and as she begins her mission, she's joined by her curious partner, 9S.

Their attempt to follow their directives is hindered by the arrival of a pair of twin Machines, brothers named Adam and Eve. The twins are frighteningly intelligent with power that goes beyond any threat the YoRHa have faced before.

In the course of defeating their enemies, 2B and 9S uncover some of the most dangerous secrets of the ancient war, becoming forever linked to the fate of humanity's legacy.

The first and second playthroughs follow the respective views of 2B and 9S during an initial invasion. After opening a route for future missions, they are sent to clear out Machine threats for the Resistance, where they discover that the Machines are exploring human societies and concepts.

The two androids work with a pacifist Machine group led by Pascal to battle Adam and Eve, physical manifestations of the Machine Network who reveal that their creators were destroyed centuries ago.

And that's just to get things started. The game continues its complex story as the player plays and fails time and again. You navigate through a twisting narrative maze that will make your head spin with the challenging story concepts, and your thumbs will ache as you play gameplay that matches its difficulty step by step.

What Did You Think of This Story?

Some of the games in this book are so innovative that they honestly can't be covered in written form. I know that sounds hyperbolic, but in the case of a game like *NieR: Automata*, there are so many twists and turns, unique endings, and complex variations only unlocked through failing other story paths, etc., that you'd need graphs and maps galore just to find your way through to the end.

NieR: Automata is an emotionally complex and philosophically rich narrative, which incidentally is about complex emotions and philosophy in software. It's a story about free will, the chase for understanding, and literally fighting for your beliefs. But when those beliefs are yanked out from under you, you find yourself searching for meaning in a godless universe, providing shades of nihilism.

The entire game is packed with references to philosophers, which add both depth and confusion to this lyrical, multipath masterpiece, and has more written about it than just about any game in modern history. Seriously, dig around, and your mind will be blown. I don't want to spoil the ending, because it really needs to be experienced to be understood, but let me just say this. You'll begin to think that machines have emotions and that androids can love and hurt and build and destroy.

And just when you think the game is done teaching you all it has to offer, *NieR: Automata* presents you with the most thought-provoking, playable end credits in gaming. I'm *not* being hyperbolic here. Trust me.

This epic tale drops you off with a hint of hope that maybe, just maybe, there are others out there in the world who are willing to make sacrifices for the benefit of humanity, and it gives you the opportunity to do the same.

NieR: Automata is one of the best play experiences I've ever had. Not only is the combat engaging and difficult, but the game isn't afraid to break the mold and shift to a totally different game format if it adds context to the story. One moment you're dancing to the death with a robotic opera boss, the next you're stuck in an isometric bullet-hell game that'll make you tear your hair out.

This game is a masterpiece. If you're up for a real brain twister combined with gameplay that will test you, then do yourself a favor and give this game a try. And don't worry, I'll be there at the end if you need a helping hand.

Celeste

Tone (N.)

The overall mood or message of a story. It can be established through a variety of means, including characterizations, pace, difficulty, visuals, symbolism, and themes.

This is it, Madeline.

Just breathe.

Why are you so nervous?

THESE ARE THE FIRST WORDS MADELINE SPEAKS to herself. A few lines of dialogue at the start of the 2D platformer, *Celeste*, that will grow in meaning as the game goes on. The colorful, pixelated protagonist enters the game at an apparent dead end, a snowy landscape decorated by a broken road sign and haphazard lampposts.

The first character she meets, even before she reaches the base of the titular mountain, is a crow. The bird awaits Madeline, perched on the edge of an icy block topped with snow. It caws as she approaches. A quick tap on the controller and Madeline attempts to bridge the gap between them. She doesn't have enough momentum to make the jump, and the game freezes. She looks up as the crow provides the next clue. Hold LT + UP to climb. Her first challenge, and yours, as you climb the small cliff. But before you can approach the crow, it flies away, leaving you alone in the snow once again.

The music seems to swirl around you like the snow that is softly falling. The tone set by this slow and quiet opening—starting at a dead end, lonely, cold—is an unwelcome beginning to what will become a difficult, almost insurmountable challenge ahead.

There's no turning back, so you follow the crow, taking over the persona of the small red-headed wanderer. Soon, you meet an old woman, Granny, standing in front of her log cabin. Madeline asks Granny if this is the way to the mountain trail, and Granny tells her it's just over the bridge. Before leaving, Madeline mentions that the driveway to Granny's house is a mess and that she should probably tell someone. Granny replies, "If my driveway almost did you in, the mountain might be a bit much for you."

Celeste © Matt Makes Games

Madeline responds defensively with an angry look on her face. "Well, if an old bat like you can survive out here, I think I'll be fine." A warning from Granny comes next, saying that Celeste Mountain is a strange place and that she might see things. Things she might not be ready to see. Madeline scoffs again, rudely, suggesting the old woman should seek help. An odd premonition, or perhaps even a bit of a look into what lies ahead for our protagonist.

This first challenge, a simple verbal taunt, requires nothing from the player. No button presses, no decisions to make. But Madeline's defensive response gives us a bit of insight into who she is. While she might come off as rough and persistent, her posture gives away that there is more to her character than meets the eye. She lacks self-esteem, a common result of dealing with anxiety and depression.

The old woman's cackling laughter floats in the air and pushes Madeline to move on. Approaching the base of Celeste Mountain, she whispers a few encouraging words to herself.

"You can do this."

Madeline crosses the threshold and begins her ascent. The game is great at introducing new challenges one at a time as you progress deeper into the experience, or in this instance, farther up the mountain. You traverse through complex, abstract obstacles as you jump, climb, glide, and run through the 2D world. The gameplay style is called platforming, and it was made popular in the eighties and nineties with games like *Mario Bros.*, *Sonic the Hedgehog*, and *Donkey Kong*. These games run the gamut from simple to unfairly complicated, and *Celeste* uses this difficulty curve within the game to emphasize difficult story points and internal conflict.

It is worth pointing out that the gameplay in this early stage of

Celeste is actually just buttery goodness and fun. Obstacles seem to be placed exactly where you need them, and the puzzle solving is logical and satisfying. That's about to change.

Madeline, a little winded but fulfilled, eventually meets another traveler at a resting place. He's young and bright, and he's set up a camp for the evening by a crackling fire. The music changes, lifting the mood slightly, as Madeline considers approaching the stranger. The fire he sits beside seems nice. The color contrast is refreshing; the rest of the world has been challenging, blue, covered with snow and ice, but his cozy, fire-lit base is inviting.

A bit of small talk follows, uncomfortable at first, but after a while, even our misplaced Madeline warms up a little. The traveler, whose name is Theo, says the mountain is difficult, almost hard to believe it even exists. And Madeline responds that it is, but perhaps that is exactly what she is looking for.

Madeline tells him she's going to the summit of Celeste Mountain. In contrast to Granny, Theo is encouraging and says that he can see determination in her eyes and that he believes she can do it. Madeline isn't quite so sure, and once again we see her self-doubt creep in. But after a bit more talk, she leaves Theo behind and continues her journey in earnest.

The simple platforming mentioned earlier begins to ramp up as Madeline makes her way to a memorial, shaped like a gravestone— a recognizable, iconic image—that reads: CELESTE MOUNTAIN—THIS MEMORIAL DEDICATED TO THOSE WHO PERISHED ON THE CLIMB.

Exhausted, Madeline manages to make a small fire for herself, then rest. She sits by the fire as the crow returns in this quiet moment. She speaks out loud to the crow her innermost fear.

"This might have been a mistake."

The screen focuses in on Madeline, a circle closing in that feels claustrophobic until the scene goes black.

She wakes in the same place, but things have changed. The warm fire, orange and crackling, has turned bluish-green, and the persistent snow has been replaced by purple falling stars. If you try to read the monument again, the letters are backward and scrambled. Something is not quite right. As you continue on, climbing this strange new mountain, you find a cave containing something unexpected. A large mirror awaits in the center of the room. Madeline finds her reflection in the mirror, but the reflection is not normal. Instead of her bright orange hair, the reflection's hair is purple, and instead of Madeline's dark eyes, the eyes in the mirror glow red.

Madeline is perplexed by this odd stranger in the mirror. It's scary. Not quite terrifying, but worrisome nonetheless. As she peers closer to study the differences in her shadow's appearance, the mirror cracks, and the other Madeline, the dark one, Madeline's self-doubt in the flesh, escapes from the mirror and dashes ahead, flying up the mountain.

Invigorated, and determined to understand more about the dark apparition, Madeline gives chase. The tempo of the music grows, and the game ramps up in difficulty. The intense things that Madeline is dealing with internally are imitated by the introduction of new obstacles in the platformer world. Now, not only is she climbing a mountain, she's also chasing a visual representation of her darkest self, and that darkest self is relentless.

After traversing through a few of the mountain's tricky rooms, she finally catches up to her dark twin for a short conversation, during which the twin speaks out. Friendly at first. "Madeline, darling. Slow down."

Madeline turns around and looks toward her bony companion as she asks, "Who said that?"

The dark twin responds with the line: "Oh, I'm simply a concerned observer." Her eyes flicker a brighter red, and she begins to float in the air. Madeline, more than a little freaked out about this, asks the other, "Are you . . . me?" And the other replies with the name she'll be known as from this point forward, "I'm Part of You."

Some reviewers have suggested that the reflection in the mirror is her id come to life. That part inside each of us that lives on instinct, impulse, and the primary of processes. I can see how that interpretation makes sense. However, I think there's something even more personal inside the reflection. Something more dangerous. To me, I see Madeline's self-doubt.

So, plotwise, you know, one event affecting the next, one could argue that this story so far is good but maybe not great. It's compelling, there's no doubt, and the idea of facing one's fears in a manifested twin is cool and unique but maybe not legendary. And that was the promise of this book, right? Not just good stories, but the greatest ever played. So what is it about this game that demands it make the cut?

To me, it's two things, and both of them would be very difficult to pull off in any other medium. One is that ramp-up of gameplay getting more difficult as the game progresses. This is very game-specific, but it isn't new. Games have done that for decades. What makes *Celeste* special is how that difficulty ties together with the story, with the realization that Madeline is trying to cope with her anxiety.

And two, the constant failure you experience as you try to complete a level is going to fill you with frustration and a desire to throw the controller down and give up. But the more you try, the more you will find little mechanisms of play, patterns you can rely on, small variants in the way you approach the game puzzle, until finally what once seemed impossible can seem . . . well, doable. It's a physical manifestation of a coping mechanism, similar to the real-life struggles many of us face today, expressed in a beautiful format that allows us to experiment and experience the satisfaction of overcoming an obstacle.

Speaking of coping mechanisms, there's a point in the game where Part of Me makes a gondola rock dangerously and we get to experience Madeline having a panic attack. The screen begins to change. Vision becomes blurry. And the music changes and distorts.

Celeste © Matt Makes Games

Then Theo teaches Madeline a technique to deal with her episode. She must control her breath and focus to keep an imaginary feather afloat. The game actually hands control over to the player in the moment, asking them to move the controller up and down to keep a feather in the middle of a small box until the rocking of the gondola slows down, the music returns to normal, and Madeline is in command of her faculties again.

Matt Makes Games, the developers of *Celeste*, uses every tool in the box to create an atmosphere that heightens the experience of dealing with anxiety. As we play, we learn to survive as Madeline through a constant series of failures. Trial and error, with an emphasis on error. The music, which is nothing short of brilliant, by the way, pushes us into uncomfortable, discordant moments, where we long for musical resolution as unfamiliar chords and melodies taunt us with unresolved sentences. The visual style of the game alternates between comfortable, welcoming areas and harsh, deadly spikes that threaten to end Madeline with every wrong twitch on the controller.

Okay, admission time. I've dealt with anxiety and depression all my life. This game speaks to me at a level that is hard to define in words. There were times when I felt that giving up was the best way for me to release this story from my mind, but it seemed as though every time I was ready to do that, the world relaxed and the gameplay simplified just enough for me to find a moment of focus. To cope.

The parallels between how the game expressed what it felt like to deal with anxiety and my own experience are real. They are instructive. They allow us to see, feel, and empathize with what it is like to feel self-doubt, anxiety, and depression in a way that no other medium can approach.

That's why *Celeste* is in this book. Because not only is this a fantastic story, it's a fantastic experience that must be played to appreciate. In great moments of pain and weakness, we have all told ourselves to give up. The scale at which that happens varies, but when Part of Me tells you to stop, it is difficult not to listen. Especially when the going gets rough.

Part of Me does her best to discourage Madeline from going on. She tells her she's not a mountain climber. She tells her to be reasonable for once. All these things are placed here to build good internal conflict. She literally tells Madeline that she can't handle this new challenge of climbing Celeste Mountain. Madeline, determined, chirps back, "That's exactly why I need to do this," and asks Part of Me, "Are you the weak part of me, or the lazy?" Not wanting to give up, Madeline defiantly continues the game, fleeing away. But as she does, the shadow gives chase. Determined, Madeline eventually escapes from Part of Me, once again finding herself alone. This is such an interesting display, because at this point, Madeline doesn't recognize or attempt to reconcile with her struggles. She literally runs away from them, pushing them out of her mind.

At its core, *Celeste* is about a young girl who doesn't just want, but *needs*, to climb a mountain. And she honestly doesn't even know why she wants to climb it. She, like most of us, can feel that something is off, but she can't quite put her finger on what is causing her malaise.

Who hasn't felt that need to just simply do something because you think it will remedy the evasive feeling that something isn't right? You have to do something new. Something . . . different to try to get out of the rut that pulled you down. Right from the get-go, I felt attached to Madeline, because she was searching for change in herself. She was searching for a challenge. I get that desire. I *feel* that need.

From the moment Madeline met Granny for the first time and heard that the mountain was a strange place, followed by the line, "You might see things you ain't ready to see," I was committed. I had to see the things the old woman warned me about and see if they affected me personally. I wanted, much like Madeline, that challenge. To look inside this game, stare Celeste Mountain right in the eyes, and see if I was ready to face what it had to offer.

Turns out, I was, and I wasn't. This game hit me like a ton of feathers. Light, almost unnoticeable, but still a *ton* of feathers.

When I first met Part of Me in the mirror, I thought it was simply interesting. I wondered if I'd have to learn to operate the game with a new set of mechanics, if I'd be asked to control this other, dark version of Madeline, but it was so much more compelling to shortly discover that this Part of Me was going to be there simply to voice my character's, and consequently my own, concerns and worries. When she suggested that I wasn't a mountain climber, that I wasn't good enough to finish this game, I honestly agreed with her.

Okay, being that I'm all about self-admissions lately, here's another one. I'm a gamer, as you have probably guessed by now. But platformers are not my forte. Puzzle games, first-person shooters, real-time strategy games—no problem. I'll make my way through. But when this game called me out by way of this odd, purple-haired, red-eyed devil, I thought, "Yeah. I'm not going to make it."

That parallel between Madeline's determination to go on and Part of Me's insistence that I couldn't make it echoed in my brain at a deep level. And as I failed over and over to fight my way through the game, two things kept me going. The story was so compelling that I had to see the top of that darned mountain, and the four words Madeline spoke at the very beginning. "You can do this."

But it wasn't just the game that haunted me. I'd felt the same way Madeline had felt most of my life. I've often felt as though I wasn't a good enough writer. A good enough artist. A good enough game developer. A dad, a son, a friend . . . the list goes on. There's always a part of me that says my goals are unachievable. That my ideals are too high. That I just don't belong.

That I am a fraud.

I knew exactly how Madeline felt, and I made finishing this game my personal mountain.

The game handles this sense of connection brilliantly by providing Part of Me as a metaphor for our inner self struggling to be freed, by presenting the metaphor as a literal expression as Part of Me and Madeline separate. Madeline, in the game, gets to play the good role, while Part of Me plays the bad. And Madeline doesn't have to blame herself for the mistakes Part of Me makes. If only real life were so simple.

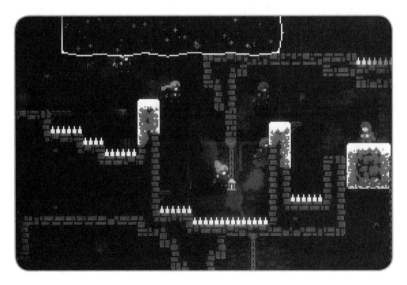

Celeste © Matt Makes Games

And it turns out, neither is the game. The more Madeline ignores Part of Me, the more she tries to run away from her and continue on without learning what she needs to do to accept her, the more intense and foreboding the game becomes.

Eventually, Madeline reaches the Mirror Temple, a new chapter filled with mirrors and green flames. The game's lore tells us that anyone who enters the Mirror Temple sees things that live within them or are created by their own mind. Every enemy that is there trying to kill Madeline is a physical reflection of her own psyche, and therefore the wounds are self-inflicted.

At this point in the game, Madeline is feeling frustrated. You can read it in her language and see it in her posture. And as the gamer, you can't help but feel the same. Madeline, when confronted by Part of Me, asks, "If you're Part of Me, why do you want to hurt me?" It's a good question. A great one, actually. And Part of Me gives an answer Madeline is "not ready to see."

Madeline thinks she doesn't need Part of Me in her life anymore. She states she wants to set her free. But the game makes it clear that that strategy is never going to work by tossing Madeline down the mountain, where she hits literal rock bottom. It's a pivotal moment in Madeline's character development, where she finally decides after trying unsuccessfully for so long to learn how to progress *with* Part of Me, not despite her.

It was eye-opening for me. A truly meaningful moment when the game explained that the only way I was going to complete this game was to learn to stop being angry with Part of Me. That Madeline needed to learn to understand that Part of Me (her) and not be angry when she arrived.

But, as is so often the case, that part of us that gives us self-doubt, the part of us that *is* depression, or anxiety, or fear, whatever it is that holds us back is often hesitant to let the learning begin. The game handles this beautifully by presenting Madeline's desire to learn to work with Part of Me and accept their differences in the form of an epic, and very challenging, boss battle. Reversing roles, where Madeline has been running away from Part of Me, Madeline chases Part of Me through the final chapter of the game as she tries to bring her close. To overcome their animosity. To become one with this important fact of what makes Madeline whole. Never before have I experienced a story that transcribed to me the feelings I have about myself in my day-to-day life in such a profound way and has given me so much hope for my own future, that everything is going to be okay. I just have to keep going.

Okay, I've internalized the heck out of this story. And I know I'm not alone here. And there's more to the story, the wrap-up after the big fight. But I honestly think it is something you might want to discover on your own, so I'm not going to spoil it. It isn't an earth-shattering revelation. It isn't a ballet of complex, acrobatic gameplay. It isn't loud, or celebratory, or particularly heroic.

But I can tell you this. The view is worth the climb, and I promise. You can do this.

BOOK REPORT:

To the Moon

To the Moon © Freebird Games

INITIAL RELEASE DATE AND PLATFORM:

November 2011 for Windows PC

WHERE ELSE CAN IT BE FOUND?

After a successful launch, Freebird Games, the makers of *To the Moon*, ported the project to Mac OS, iOS, Linux, Android, and the Nintendo Switch, where it can be found today.

Category:

Linear Narrative, Action/Adventure

Main Characters:

Johnny Wyles, our dying protagonist, who wants nothing more than to meet his sweetheart on the moon

River Wyles, Johnny's wife and love of his life, who has previously passed

Dr. Eva Rosalene and Dr. Neil Watts, scientists and doctors employed by Sigmund Corp. to deliver wish-fulfillment dreams

Setting:

The game begins at the entrance of Johnny Wyles's mansion, but soon we are transported to the past as we revisit the memories of the dying man.

Story Summary:

In the not-so-distant future, Sigmund Corp. invents a technology that can create artificial memories. But since the false memories create problems with a person's actual memories, this "wish fulfillment" service is only offered to those on their deathbeds.

Two Sigmund Corp. doctors, Dr. Eva Rosalene and Dr. Neil Watts, are contracted to fulfill the lifelong dream of the dying Johnny Wyles. Johnny wants to go to the moon. Before they can honor his wishes, the doctors need to discover why. Using "mementos" from Johnny's life, items of great personal significance to Johnny that act as a link between significant memories, the two doctors travel back into his memories, and with each leap they discover more about Johnny and his link to the most important person in his life, his wife, River.

Through memories implanted in Johnny, he and River are allowed to relive their lives as they learn that sometimes it is the journey, not the destination, that provides true happiness.

WHAT DID YOU THINK OF THIS STORY?

I guess part of what I loved was the universality of wanting to go back and revisit things we might have done better in the past. I mean, who hasn't wanted to correct a thing or two from time to time. But I think it was the building of the relationship between River and Johnny that truly captured me. *To the Moon* is a sweet romance, but so much more as we discover that every encounter in our lives is precious and that we should not take these passing moments for granted.

This game has its roots exposed as we play through what could probably best be called a visual text adventure game, but there are enough aspects of mystery and simple puzzle games mixed in to make you feel invested in Johnny's dream to go to the moon with his wife. *To the Moon* is bittersweet, nostalgic, and perfectly beautiful all at the same time.

Theme

Theme (N.)

A theme is a universal idea, lesson, or message explored throughout a work of literature. One key characteristic of literary themes is their universality, which is to say that themes are ideas that not only apply to the specific characters and events of a book or play but also express broader truths about human experience that readers can apply to their own lives.

AVE YOU EVER HAD YOUR FORTUNE READ? I HAVE, although I don't believe in that stuff in the slightest. But considering how our species evolved, I'd wager that everyone would jump at the chance to know precisely what their fortune bears. Even if it were bad news. If you knew your car wasn't going to start in the morning before you left for work, you could at least plan for it. Unfortunately, as far as I know, no one has figured this out quite yet. Perhaps one day our AI overlords will solve the little problem of worldwide unpredictability for us. But in the meantime, before that dreadful day when everything is known and our lives are meticulously planned for us from birth until death, we can continue to wonder *what if?*

The unexpected stokes human imagination because we want to be prepared for every possible scenario. Part of the pleasure in having your fortune told is the anticipation *before* you hear: "Something you've misplaced will reappear again soon," or "a secret admirer will send you a sign of their affection." And then anxiously waiting the following days for your wallet to pop up out of nowhere, or for when that stranger you've shared glances with dramatically follows you on Instagram. And it's not just waiting to find out what good tidings fate may bring that engages us. Fearing misfortune does this as well.

We had to evolve to respond quickly to the unexpected because our world is so unpredictable. Even the most certain things have a chance of turning on their head and surprising everyone. The only thing we can be certain of is how uncertain everything is. Our minds are trained to respond to pay attention to the unforeseen, because the one time you turn your back to the good ole watering hole is when you're snatched up by a crocodile. Everyone knows the sun is going to rise tomorrow morning, just as it has for the past . . . let me check my calendar . . . billions of years. You could spend every waking moment horrified about what would happen if it suddenly fell out of the sky, but why bother when there are so many other things more likely to change? The things we have come to learn won't ever change fall into our subconscious. We don't even think about them, so we can spend our energy worrying about things we know are uncertain.

Stories are a powerful tool for playing out those *what if?* scenarios. A character faces an unavoidable challenge, and they have to navigate through it. It's the first form of virtual reality. One that runs on a script and uses the mind as a processor. Stories can warn us of physical danger and social pitfalls.

In a way, getting your fortune told is like a little story. Really! If you believe in it, and the fortune is ambiguous enough, then you won't be able to keep yourself from daydreaming about what you will do when the moment comes. "When my wallet reappears, I am going straight to the mall to get a new PlayStation 5." Or, "When that gorgeous stranger finally professes their love, I'm going to have the perfect, most enchanting response. Something like, 'Do you have a PlayStation 5?'"

We've established why the unexpected grabs our attention and how stories can help us envision the future to prepare for those events. And I've already talked about when a character faces a challenging obstacle and how they change because of it, but if a story were just a series of unusual, eye-catching external events with no direction, then being a storyteller would be much easier. There is no limit to the combination of wacky, inane ideas you could slap on top of one another. But, as trivial as it sounds, that wouldn't be a story at all. Without a point to work toward, a story becomes an endless series of random *what ifs?* until it just sort of . . . ends.

What we want from stories is direction.

Coming up with a compelling *what if this cool thing happened?* is a skill in and of itself and is an important part of getting our attention, but that is just the first step. Everyone knows a book, a movie, or a video game that enthralled them in the beginning with a gripping *what if* but felt left in the dust as the story went on. What happened to all that momentum? Instead of feeling rewarded and energized by a tale well told, you feel betrayed by something you spent too much time on, hoping it would turn around for the better.

A story has impact when that gripping *what if* and those interesting events aren't just surprising, but meaningful. Meaningful to the characters. A good plot forces a character to confront uncomfortable truths and change because of them. Our brains are connected to stories because we want to learn from them, to plan for the future. So it makes sense that the characters in the story would learn something, too, from an event they didn't expect. Ultimately, what stories build up to, and what we are waiting for as the audience, is the conclusion of the protagonist's journey. The moment when they see the world differently from when they started. It's the responsibility of a storyteller to stick the landing. And that doesn't happen by accident. The storyteller designed everything from head to toe: the plot, the sensory details, the designs, the backstory, all point to the theme.

Like a painting, the composition of the piece is carefully planned to draw the eye to one point, the focal point.

When you identify the theme in a piece of work, you will begin to notice other parts of the story that support that message. And that is when knowing literary devices comes in handy. The more familiar you are with them, the more you'll begin to spot stories that use them. Like metaphor, parallel narratives, foreshadowing, symbolism, contrast, etc. For example, in the well-known people-simulator game *The Sims*, we might think the game is about architecture and building happy lives and creating personal narratives for your Sims. But as the game progresses, you discover that relationships are at the core of every design feature in the game. The relationship you have with the Sim you created. The relationship your Sim has to the items you purchase and careers you choose for them. The relationship of your Sim to other Sims in the game world. The more the focus is on this critical part of the story, the more meaningful it is to you as the player when those relationships change.

The challenges the character faces along the way before realizing the theme is internal conflict. The more frequently the story touches on how the character feels or thinks about what they are struggling with internally, the better. The audience can get inside that person's head and feel their struggle as if it were their own. The more relevant the answer, the more rewarding the experience.

Theme is one of the reasons people like stories for different reasons. The theme of a story may be very relevant to you, but to someone else, it might not resonate at all. Gamers, readers, and reviewers often debate what theme the creator originally intended, but, in the end, I don't think that really matters. The only thing that should matter is what the story meant to you.

BOOK REPORT:

What Remains of Edith Finch

What Remains of Edith Finch © Giant Sparrow

INITIAL RELEASE DATE AND PLATFORM:

April 2017 for Windows PC

Where Else Can It Be Found?

Ports of this game can be found on the Nintendo Switch, PlayStation 4, and Xbox One.

Category:

Linear Narrative, Action/Adventure, first person exploration game

Main Characters:

Edith Finch, our main character and the last living member of the tragically cursed Finch family

Setting:

You explore the Finch house and surrounding wilderness through a series of rooms, footpaths, and secret crawl spaces. Players are guided through the house by Edith as she narrates her thoughts, which are also visually displayed to the player as part of the scene to direct the player's attention. Through the house, you encounter a series of memorials to deceased relatives. Players make progress by interacting with these shrines and experiencing vignettes of the relative's death. Each flashback varies in gameplay genre and visual style.

Story Summary:

Edith Finch has returned to her family home to learn about the fates of the four generations who lived there over the past century. The house was expanded as the family grew, forming a twisting path of hidden corridors and bedrooms, each unique and distinct. In a perfect example of environmental storytelling, this paints a picture of the family members without overexplaining things, letting our imagination fill in the gaps as we explore the belongings strewn across the floor, pinned to walls, and resting on nightstands of those who have passed away. As Edith explores the Finch household, she reads stories and things come to life as we learn how the supposed family curse affected each and every member of Edith's family tree.

The ancestors' stories are where the game shines. No two tales are the same, each told in a way that perfectly matches the voice of the character at its center. You will learn about Edith's relatives through poems, letters, or diaries, taking advantage of each of the format's strengths while celebrating other storytelling mediums. It weaves tried and tested forms of writing together to fabricate a unique and wonderful style all its own. The stories also do not make you a passive observer but instead involve you in their plots. Whether that be flying a kite, attacking a seal as a great white shark, or taking pictures in the forest, you take part in how every tale plays out.

WHAT DID YOU THINK OF THIS STORY?

Surprisingly, even though it is one of the best examples of showing, not telling, a story that I've ever seen, the point of this game is not about exploring the environment to decipher the backstory of this eclectic house's inhabitants. *What Remains of Edith Finch* is about family. About how even if we haven't met the members of our family tree, they can still affect our lives. As she journeys through the house, we see how each person from her past has profoundly affected who she has become.

The way Edith's story is told is just as beautiful as each tale of loss she reads. Her own feelings are written ahead of you, floating in the air or wrapped around an important piece of furniture as you wander through the house, adding context to her surroundings and helping her understand the people who once called it home. Doing things like pushing open doors or staring out windows to the sea makes each sentence bend, flow, and twist like a living novel, yet the text is positioned perfectly so that you don't miss a word. The way in which Edith's thoughts are presented to us, piece by piece, and the pitch-perfect voice performance connect each story and make every tale even more special. The writing is exceptional, packing an incredible amount of thought and emotion into short, meaningful sentences.

Each story is told as an allegory, letting us know how each character died, yet never quite showing the final moment, leaving our imagination to fill the gaps. The tone isn't sad or depressing but playful and celebratory—skipping the stages of grief and denial and going straight to acceptance. Since Edith isn't overcome with sadness at the events of each tale, our feelings are spared as well. Instead, I wished I knew each member of the Finch family better and could learn even more about their lives.

The end of the game is just as powerful as each of the individual tales. It would diminish the impact to explain exactly what happens once Edith knows everyone's story, but there is an understanding, a fateful shadow lingering that gradually makes its presence clearer as you progress through the game. It's yet another gripping thread that Edith must come to accept, just like everything else in the game, and that thread proves to be just as beautiful, if not more so, as everything that came before.

The Last of Us

Chiasmus (N.)

A reversal in the order of words in two otherwise parallel phrases, as in "He went to the country, to the town went he." Latin for cross, this can also refer to a more global switch of two story elements, with a centralized point where the two collide.

T HE *LAST OF US* BEGINS IN SEPTEMBER 2013, WITH father and daughter, Joel and Sarah. We can tell at once that all they have is each other. There isn't a trace of Sarah's mother to be found in the house. After a hard day of work, Joel lumbers in late one night and plops down on the couch next to Sarah, who stayed up late for him. She gives her dad a present for his birthday, a wristwatch (which will become an important icon throughout the series), and he playfully teases her that it doesn't work before the two settle in to watch a little TV.

Moments later, Joel takes sleepy Sarah in his arms and packs her up to bed (another motif that we'll return to more than once, and a visual example of her dependence on him and his willingness to play that role).

It is this, the first night of the outbreak, that will define their lives. Something urges Sarah to wake up after a few hours, still late in the night. She stumbles around looking for her father before discovering some disturbing clues that shock her awake. A broadcast on the news, an explosion in the city close enough to see from her upstairs window, a bunch of missed calls on Joel's phone, but Joel himself is nowhere to be seen.

As things get more intense, the game steals control away from the player and shows us the first of many murders. Joel, a man obviously prepared for a situation like this, bursts in through a sliding glass door and slams it shut, breathing heavily. He commands Sarah to step back, but she is frozen in fear. Joel shouts another warning, this time at something outside the house, then he pulls out a handgun from a desk drawer. A shady figure approaches the house, ignoring Joel's warning. The intruder, driven mad with bloodlust, crashes through the glass, shattering the silence forever on what was once the peaceful life in the suburbs. Moments before Joel is overwhelmed, he opens fire on the monster that was once their neighbor, Jimmy.

The next fifteen or so minutes are pandemonium. Sarah, frightened and confused, hastily follows her protector outside as he tries to explain to her in as comforting a voice as possible why they need to leave town. Joel's brother, Tommy, is already waiting for them in the driveway, anxiously calling for them to hop inside his SUV.

The family drives through a city in flames, muscling their way through the clogged traffic and chaotic crowds. After finally breaking through the worst of the mess, Tommy rounds a corner and is T-boned by a speeding vehicle. The screen goes black. Joel blinks open bleary eyes and tries to make sense of his upside-down world. He snaps back to reality and worriedly checks on Sarah in the back seat and finds her nursing a broken leg. Joel kicks out the windshield, crawls out, and gingerly pulls his daughter through behind him.

Joel hands Tommy his weapon and asks his brother to defend them as he carries Sarah in his arms through the outskirts of the city, echoing his action from earlier. But this time, instead of walking her sleepy body to the sanctuary of her bedroom, Joel is carrying her through a horde of zombies, panicked people, and lastly to a military roadblock where we find ourselves at the crux of the inciting incident.

Joel carrying Sarah in The Last of Us © Naughty Dog

Desperate and exhausted, the survivors reach the last leg of their mad dash out of the infected city, a mile away from any streetlights or watchful eyes. It's just them and a lone soldier, decked head to toe in military-grade quarantine gear. Joel begs for assistance, asking for a doctor to look at his daughter's leg. The faceless soldier dips his head to listen to a fuzzy radio strapped to his shoulder, then utters a brisk affirmative. He lifts up his assault rifle, takes aim at the unarmed, defenseless pair, and fires. Joel and Sarah are struck, and Joel collapses. Tommy catches up behind them just in time to kill the soldier and save Joel's life, but he is too late to rescue his niece.

This is the third and final instance of Joel's clutching Sarah to his chest. He pleads for her to hold on, but there is nothing anyone can do to help her. We're left with a shot of the wristwatch on his arm as we first hear the haunting, quiet, efficient notes of a guitar pick out a somber melody, what we will come to recognize as Joel's Theme.

I kind of dropped and glossed over a term there that needs a little explanation, because it is really important to storytelling. The inciting incident, the death of Joel's daughter. In a nutshell, the inciting incident is a narrative event that launches the main action. This is a well-accepted definition, but I think there's one other aspect that is often overlooked. Not only should this event launch the main action, but, in my opinion, it also needs to set the main character on a path that they will never be able to return from. From this point on, everything changes. We can never go back.

Okay, that might sound a little strong, but I find that the most compelling inciting incidents include this nothing-will-ever-be-the-same aspect. And in this case, Joel's case, that is exactly what has happened. Losing Sarah, holding her in his arms as she passes away, is something that changes Joel's life forever.

The game picks up again twenty years later. Human civilization has been all but extinguished because of the viral outbreak. Joel, once a hardworking family man, has become a professional smuggler. He has turned inward, isolating himself emotionally and focusing his efforts on surviving in their harsh world.

Joel's closest friend, a coworker named Tess, who's as tough as nails, asks for his help on a potential mission. Marlene, the leader of an antigovernment faction called the Fireflies, requests they transport a young girl named Ellie to a base in Colorado, where they are researching a cure for the global infection. It's no easy task. The last two decades of the apocalypse eroded society at an alarming rate, allowing Mother Nature to dominate and crack infrastructure. What's more, Joel later finds out his baggage, Ellie, isn't a regular fourteen-year-old. Rather, she may be the key to a possible vaccine, evidenced by the fact that she didn't turn after getting bitten by one of the infected. This makes her a highly valuable asset and will draw more unwanted attention on their trek from the East Coast to the Midwest through maverick factions of wanton outlaws and cannibals, not to mention the hordes of zombies who have been gradually mutating in the dark for the past twenty years.

The three begin their journey by escaping their tightly sealed government quarantine zone. They fail to slip through the defenses undetected, and military personnel in armored vehicles, hot on their trail, pin them down in what appears to have once been some kind of large government building that has lost its luster to the passage of time and exposure to the elements. When it is obvious they are trapped, Tess offers to stay behind and shoot it out so Joel and Ellie can dash out the back. Joel and Ellie try to persuade her to do otherwise, but she reveals that she's been bitten and that she wants to go out on her own terms. Fighting for something she believes in.

Tess's sacrifice gives Joel and Ellie the time they need to escape the military. Joel begins to question the purpose of completing the journey. While he has tried to close his heart to emotion, Tess's death obviously affects him. It's another person he felt responsible for but couldn't protect in the end, and he hates himself for caring for her in the first place.

Joel and Ellie brawl their way through various fungal-faced baddies. Joel wants to find a fellow smuggler who owes him a favor, but the last time they saw each other they didn't part on very good terms. He locates the paranoid loner, Bill, only after triggering a few of his well-laid lethal traps. Joel cashes in his favor, and Bill reluctantly agrees. Whatever Joel did for the bitter, manic survivor in the past must have meant a lot to him, because he's willing to risk his life. Bill helps them get an old truck up and running again, but they have to sneak and battle their way through a horde of infected to get a new battery. After a few close calls, and a million grumbling complaints from Bill, they start the truck, and Joel and Ellie make their way to Pittsburgh. But not before Bill takes Joel aside and shares his cautionary tale. Bill lost his only friend and lover, Frank. He urges Joel to learn from his greatest mistake and warns him not to get too close to Ellie. The remark reminds Joel of the people in his life he's lost to the apocalypse. Not the least of which is his daughter, who Ellie shares a bit of a resemblance with.

During the long road trip, Joel and Ellie connect a little more. Ellie admits she is a bit of a kleptomaniac and dumps her bulging backpack, full of all the treasures she swiped from Bill's hideout, onto the back seat. Joel, a little impressed, tries to hide his grin behind a reprimand. It's impossible not to like the little firecracker. Ellie notices she is finally starting to get through Joel's rough exterior and tries to broach the topic of Tess's death, but Joel shuts down fast like an iron gate.

Moments like these show just how skilled Naughty Dog is at delivering heartwarming dialogue and ending it with a taste of the internal conflict the protagonist is experiencing. It's a well-balanced concoction of sweet and sour, a much-needed bit of sugar to help the medicine go down.

The bright moment is cut short when they enter Pittsburgh and are ambushed by the Hunters, a brutal gang of cannibals infamous for attacking anyone who steps on their territory. Ellie and Joel recover from the loss of their vehicle and shortly after stumble on another pair of survivors trying to escape the Hunters as well. Their two new companions, Sam and Henry, are brothers. And for a time, it seems as though having strength in numbers proves a viable strategy. Sam and Ellie share a moment when she steals a toy Henry won't allow the young boy to carry in his bag. But the good times don't last for long. During their skirmishes, Sam becomes infected, and Henry, his body shaking, shoots him and then takes his own life. Another substantial, sobering example to Joel of the cost of loving someone in the apocalypse.

Okay, I'm rushing through this pretty fast because there's a lot to cover, but I want to reiterate a few important things the story is doing before moving on. *The Last of Us* is not a game about mowing down hordes of zombies. It's not about scrounging for supplies to survive the apocalypse. It isn't even about finding a cure. It's about characters. What Naughty Dog does so well is make sure that every person in Joel's life plays a role in changing his story. Not only to move the plot forward in a general sense, to make the trek west more interesting, but in another, more specific, meaningful purpose.

Tess, Bill, Sam, and Henry are all stark reminders to Joel of why he runs away from personal connection. The source of his greatest fear stems from the day he lost his daughter, and the ghost of that memory haunts him daily. It's no accident that Ellie is the same age as when Sarah died, or that she looks a little like her, and that she even acts like her. It's to make spending time with her so agonizing, yet impossible for Joel to ignore. Ellie has become more than just a travel buddy, she has forced Joel to confront the loss of his daughter, once and for all. Ellie's presence could heal his broken soul, but opening up his heart again means risking losing her. And the story of every person he's met since the beginning of his expedition has tugged on his instinct to abandon Ellie for his own sake.

Joel training Ellie in The Last of Us *© Naughty Dog*

The story of *The Last of Us* flashes forward to the fall. Weeks after Sam's tragic death and his brother's suicide, the pair have traveled miles to finally find some well-deserved good fortune. They visit Tommy, Joel's brother, who is not only still alive but also prospering in an impressive settlement, where he resides with his wife and other survivalists. Even though the two travelers have grown close, Joel has kept secret a decision he made long ago about what to do with Ellie. His plan to see Tommy serves two purposes. One, to rest and refuel, and two, to leave Ellie behind. The losses they saw on their journey made up his mind for him. Remembering what it was like to lose Sarah is too unbearable, and he can't risk going through it again.

When Joel tells Ellie what he is going to do, she steals a horse and leaves the settlement on her own. Joel and Tommy charge after her, right into danger as Ellie has drawn the attention of deadly scavengers. But the bandits are simply an external danger. The true conflict takes place when they find Ellie hiding in the second story of an abandoned farmhouse. In one of the most memorable, outstanding performances in entertainment history, Joel and Ellie finally lay their feelings bare and hash things out. Ellie accuses Joel of wanting to leave her the entire time they were traveling together. It's a truth he cannot deny, and it pisses her off. Joel tries to justify his dishonesty by saying she will be safer with Tommy, but she can see right through him.

Ellie tells Joel she knows about Sarah. It strikes a sensitive nerve more painful than any bullet or bite. She tells Joel she's lost people, just like him. Joel strikes back like a cornered animal and accuses her of not having any idea what loss is. It's an extremely unfair, obstinate thing to say to a kid who has never known life outside of the apocalypse. Ellie never knew her dad, and her mother gave her up to Marlene when she was just a baby. She discovered she was immune to the infection when she and her friend were attacked. Her friend turned, but Ellie did not, and she had to kill her to survive. Marlene watched after her for a time but was later forced to ship her off with Joel and Tess. She thought Joel would be different.

The conversation morphs. Ellie doesn't just want Joel to be honest with her, she wants him to stay by her side. She's asking for him to be a father figure. But Joel isn't willing to be that vulnerable. To protect himself, he tells her that she isn't his daughter and that he will never be her dad.

Before Ellie can dash off again in a shower of tears, Tommy bursts through the door, interrupting their private moment. Reinforcements are on their way, and his wife informed him via radio they are attacking the settlement. Ellie and Joel giddyup back to base and help clear out the intruders. Tommy, grateful for their assistance, offers them a permanent home among them. But Joel, who had time to think about his interaction with Ellie, denies Tommy and asks for directions to a nearby Fireflies settlement at the University of Eastern Colorado. Ellie, pleased at his decision, returns the horse she stole and hops on the back of Joel's horse, and the two trek through the Rocky Mountains to finish their quest.

Believe it or not, this moment, a little over halfway through the story, is the last significant change in Joel's character development. And for those of you who know how this tale comes to a close and are up in arms with that controversial statement, read to the end before you disagree with me. A worse storyteller, when coming up with *The Last of Us*, could have looked at Joel's progression up until this point and thought: "This is technically complete. Joel has finally learned that it is better to have loved and lost than to never have loved at all." The moment Joel chooses to finish the journey with Ellie instead of leaving her behind with Tommy is the perfect happy ending because he allows Ellie to heal the part of himself that died when he lost Sarah. Joel gets what he wants, and Ellie gets what she wants. Then they find the Fireflies, and the virus is cured. Hooray! And *The Last of Us* would probably have floated away, adrift in the never-ending sea of forgettable zombie horror stories of the early 2010s.

But this is not where the story ends. The writers of *The Last of Us* wanted to take Joel's lesson to the extreme and show us just how bittersweet choosing to love someone could be. Over and over, we agonize with Joel's attempts to put distance between Ellie and himself, and yet we can't help but grow to love her as he does. And then, as we head into the second half of the game, Joel is injured and they reverse roles. Ellie becomes his caretaker. The provider. In many ways, the adult. The bond between them grows ever stronger. Joel and Ellie are willing to stick by each other, through thick and thin. Even though Joel was wavering about his commitment earlier, he is dedicated to his decision now.

Finally, by the springtime, a full year after they first met, and close to the end of *The Last of Us*, Joel and Ellie reach the Fireflies. They have since moved on from Colorado, and our protagonists locate them in their lab in Salt Lake City, Utah. Ellie almost drowns, and Joel begs some guards to help him revive her. They knock him out, smacking him in the head with the butt of a gun. When he wakes up, he's been taken to a facility. Marlene, the woman who originally asked him to smuggle the teen across the United States in the first place, tells him that Ellie is being prepped for surgery so they can extract the infected part of her brain they need to create a cure and that Ellie must die.

For Joel, this is unacceptable. Of all the people in the world who had to die to cure the virus—why did it have to be her? After years of having every tiny bit of joy slowly ripped away from him, he won't let them take Ellie away, too. His mind was made up months before. When he chose to take Ellie with him, he was never going to let her go.

Joel gears up once again and sets his murderous sights on the good guys, the Fireflies. He opens fire on the guards and litters the hallways of the hospital with their corpses. Covered in blood, he ferociously tears through the double doors and stabs the surgical knife the doctor is holding into his throat. The other doctors don't stand in his way—they just look on in horror as Joel scoops Ellie up in his arms from the operating table and swoops out the back.

The last obstacle in his way before he's free is Marlene. On the verge of tears, she tries to persuade Joel to return the girl, humanity's one hope at salvation. Joel shoots her in the gut and disappears into the night.

The Last of Us was the defining game of the PS3 generation, showed us how powerful the PS4 was in the remastered version, and even found its way to the PS5. It's a classic, and it has probably been covered more when it comes to storytelling in games than any other. But before we get into the grips of why it was so powerful, I want to bring up something that I can't remember happening in any other blockbuster game. Chiasmus.

No, that isn't one of the viral bugs that turns people into the infected. Chiasmus is a storytelling device, or perhaps more accurately, a storytelling structure. Chiasmus, which comes from a Greek word meaning "crossed," refers to when a grammatic structure inverts a previous phrase. That is, you say one thing, and then you say something very similar, but flipped around.

Usually, chiasmus happens on a sentence level. For example, the line "Live simply so that others might simply live," a famous quote by Gandhi. But, it can also happen on a paragraph, chapter, or even full-story level. *The Last of Us* takes this latter, more wholesale approach, and if I'm being honest, I think it's brilliant.

Let's zoom out and look at the story from the thirty-thousand-foot level. Way out here we only see the biggest plot points, and you get something like this:

- The game starts with a dependent Sarah being carried by Joel to her tragic death.
- The main conflict happens as Joel says he's going to leave Ellie behind, and she persuades him not to.
- Shortly after, we take control of Ellie as she learns more about herself and her independence.
- And last, Joel carries Ellie in his arms once again, as he carries her *away* from her death.

This cross in the plot meets in the middle when the internal conflict is at its climax. Even in a story that ends in such a dark, tragic way as *The Last of Us*, we feel transfixed, and a little comforted, by Joel's character development. And in this game, we'll take any comfort we can find.

But, not only do we see chiasmus in the swapping and crossing of plot points, we also see this in terms of vulnerability of the game's two main characters. When the game picks up twenty years after Sarah's death, Joel is completely shut off emotionally. Even when he loses Tess toward the beginning of the game, we can tell it affects him, but he doesn't speak about it.

Ellie, on the other hand, is at her most vulnerable, both physically and emotionally, as the game begins. She isn't even armed. She uses strong language to act tough, but most of the time she crouches behind Joel as he clears out a room with brute force and firepower. And in moments of high action, neither she nor Joel converse. But, in quiet moments, when action is reduced, those times between violent encounters, Ellie can't help but show us her age. While walking through an overgrown garden, she points out a gnome statue to Joel and mentions she had an art book filled with them "as a kid." Joel doesn't know how to respond. Later, we see her tiptoeing excitedly to see over a fence in an animation that can only be described as curious and playful. She learns to whistle and remarks upon it, proud of her new trick, and Joel responds with something like, "Oh good. Something else you can drive me crazy with."

These quiet moments between the two have perhaps the most impact at showing growth, and how they eventually swap places in the narrative. One of the best examples of this happening is as the two of them are sneaking through a tall apartment building. They stand at the entrance to a stairwell, and Ellie starts the short conversation. I've quoted it below.

"Hearing them talk. At least they're scared of us," Ellie says. And Joel quickly responds.

"Just try not to let your guard down."

Then Ellie shares something that's difficult for her to admit. Emotions are easier for her, but being raised during the apocalypse has had its impact. However, she is trying. Really searching for a connection with Joel as she says, "I'm just saying, it's good having you on my side."

A moment goes by as Joel doesn't respond. Then Ellie finishes the thought. "That . . . was a compliment."

And in typical Joel fashion, all he can respond with is, "Okay." A phrase we've heard him share more times than we care to count.

These small conversations are so important in building the bond between the two of them, and while dialogue like this, nonessential, ambient-style dialogue, isn't new to games, Naughty Dog uses it in such a crafty way that we can feel the two of them grow closer, and we grow closer to both of them as a result.

Now, let's contrast this conversation with their last one.

But, before we do, I just have to spend one paragraph mentioning the amazing musical score, the unparalleled art and animation, and the best voice acting in the biz. No, seriously, Troy Baker (Joel) and Ashley Johnson (Ellie) are nothing short of masters of their craft. It is the subtlety of all these amazing actors that makes the ending work. Bravo to the entire creative team here, because a century from now people will study the last three minutes of *The Last of Us* like they study Shakespeare's *King Lear*.

After Joel rescues Ellie from the lab, she wakes up in the back of a car and asks Joel what happened. He lies to her, saying they found other people who are immune but weren't able to create a vaccine, so they gave up. It's unclear if Ellie fully believes Joel's lie or if deep down she knows he spared her life at the cost of a cure.

Once again control switches from Joel to Ellie. The set has changed as the lights come up, and we find ourselves in mountains once again. Ellie follows Joel through the forest. Little to no dialogue happens for a while, until Joel extends a hand to lift Ellie up to a small plateau. We can see Joel's brother's small settlement at the bottom of the valley, and Joel begins to make his way there before Ellie stops him.

"Hey, wait," she says. Joel turns back to her, and she struggles to make eye contact. She lets out a deep sigh. We can feel the weight of the words in her mind, see it in her shoulders. Read the concern on her face. I'll let the script take it from here. I don't want to get in the way.

> Ellie: Back in Boston . . . back when I was bitten . . . I wasn't alone. My best friend was there. And she got bit, too. We didn't know what to do. So . . . she says, . . . "Let's just wait it out. Y'know, we can be all poetic and just lose our minds together." [pause] I'm still waiting for my turn.

Joel: Ellie—

Ellie: Her name was Riley, and she was the first to die. And then it was Tess. And then Sam.

Joel: None of that is on you.

Ellie: No, you don't understand.

Joel: I struggled for a long time with survivin'. And you— . . . No matter what . . . you keep finding something to fight for. Now, I know that's not what you want to hear right now, but it's—

Ellie: Swear to me. [long beat] Swear to me that everything you said about the Fireflies is true.

[Joel hesitates for a long beat]

Joel: I swear.

[Ellie distances herself for a longer beat. After a long hesitation, she looks up to Joel and finally nods.]

Ellie: . . . Okay.

Ellie confronting Joel in The Last of Us © Naughty Dog

Ellie's final word was her crossover to taking on the personality of Joel. He has become the one who needs, and she has become the emotionally shut off, tight-lipped adult. Ellie's confession about her friend Riley shows that the writers understood that her backstory was just as important as Joel's, leaving the player with another unsettling moment to ponder. When Ellie and Joel found the Fireflies, it was her decision to die on the operating table. She didn't see it as an opportunity to sacrifice herself for humanity and become some grand hero, she was getting her turn after waiting so long to die with her friend. In her words, it was the "poetic" ending she wanted after all. To Ellie, her life would have meaning.

From Ellie's point of view, Joel's final decision to save her is seen as truly selfish. Not just because of what he took away from humanity, but from what he took away from her.

This ending. Oh, this ending. It's just so hard to even discuss, because it's so full of interpretation. Not by accident, mind you. Naughty Dog deliberately leaves this game in the bravest manner, in the hands and the imagination of the player. The bond between Joel and Ellie is what makes this game tick, not the high moments of grandiose violence.

There's no doubt that when this game launched, the zombie genre was already on its last leg (figuratively, there are still plenty of legs to go around for zombies to dine on), but Naughty Dog didn't lean on the tried-and-true zombie tropes. They focused on the thing that remained, humanity. Those who survived. You know, the last of us.

And really, this is what makes what Joel did at the end of the game so difficult to process. In a game that highlights the worst and the best of what humanity has to offer, the hero of this story walks away from his chance to make a difference.

The brilliance of this story is that the writers know why we can't help but fall in love with these tragic characters, and it's because they carefully planned Joel's journey from the beginning with the end in mind. It's when we understand the context of Joel's personal history that the decision to save Ellie becomes deeply emotional. I have a daughter, two actually. I'd probably make the same weak, selfish decision Joel made. More than probably. I would. I'd save my daughters, ten times out of ten.

There is no excuse for the monster Joel has become. But at least I can empathize with why he did what he did. He learned his lesson long before Ellie was set on the operating table. To love, rather than to have never loved at all and lost. The final scenario challenged his commitment to his utmost, forcing him to do despicable things to remain true to his decision.

I mentioned earlier that we'll be looking back at this game for decades, comparing it to some of the literary greats. I truly believe that is the case. Graphics will get better. We'll change how we interface and control this technology. Our understanding of games as literature will continue to mature. But the important things, the story, the relationships, the music, the mood, will remain unchanged. They will have just as much impact tomorrow as they did when this masterpiece was shared with the world on June 14, 2013.

BOOK REPORT:

Chrono Trigger

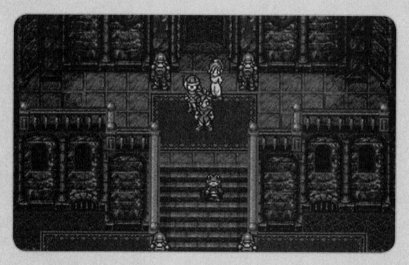

Chrono Trigger © Square Enix

INITIAL RELEASE DATE AND PLATFORM:

March 1995 for Super Nintendo Entertainment System

WHERE ELSE CAN IT BE FOUND?

Luckily for us, this game can be found on the PlayStation, Nintendo DS, Android and iPhone, Nintendo Virtual Console, and even on a Windows PC.

CATEGORY:

Nonlinear Branching Narrative, Action/Adventure RPG

MAIN CHARACTERS:

Crono, a boy with red-spiked hair. This silent protagonist shows us how to be a hero without ever speaking a word. However, his facial expressions are legendary.

Marle (Princess Nadia Marldia), the princess of Guardia

Lucca Ashtear, Crono's childhood friend

Frog, an anthropomorphic knight from the Middle Ages

Robo, a futuristic robot put out of commission in AD 1999, before being repaired by Lucca

Ayla, the chief of the prehistoric tribe

Magus, the lord of the Mystics of the Middle Ages

SETTING:

Chrono Trigger takes place in a world similar to Earth, with eras such as the prehistoric age, in which primitive humans and dinosaurs share the planet; the Middle Ages, replete with knights, monsters, and magic; and the post-apocalyptic future, where destitute humans and sentient robots struggle to survive.

STORY SUMMARY:

In AD 1000, Crono and Marle watch Lucca and her father demonstrate a new teleportation device at the Millennial Fair. When Marle volunteers to be teleported, her pendant interferes with the device and it goes wonky, sending her to another time, rather than another place. Crono and Lucca separately re-create the portal and find themselves in AD 600. They learn that Marle's presence has created a grandfather paradox by preventing the recovery of Marle's kidnapped ancestor. Crono and Lucca, with the help of Frog, restore history to normal by recovering the kidnapped woman. But their adventure has created problems in the present, and the group is forced to flee into another time portal, this time landing far in the future, where a giant creature known as Lavos has wiped out most of civilization. Right then and there, the three promise to do whatever it takes to prevent the destruction of their world.

As the game progresses, the team grows and fan favorites Ayla and Robo join in the fun. The more the group tries to clean things up, the more they play around with the time line, and the more complicated things become.

WHAT DID YOU THINK OF THIS STORY?

Time travel is a messy component to add to any story, but that doesn't mean it isn't fun. There's just something great about seeing the consequences that come from making changes to the past, and watching the results go bananas.

Chrono Trigger hops from AD 1000 to 12000 BC constantly, as you play around with one time-shifting paradox to another, in one of the most complex, yet well-thought-out examples of the troubles with time travel ever created. I've played many times, which isn't uncommon for *Chrono Trigger* fans, and each time I'm blown away with how thoughtful the developers were in trying to keep all the time lines in line and the characters engaged.

The dialogue is fun and snappy, and the whole world is filled with memorable characters. But I'd be remiss if I didn't mention that this game has thirteen very different endings. While it could be argued there are some preferred endings, *Chrono Trigger* is still held up today as an excellent example of branching narrative gaming.

God of War

Character Development (N.)

The portrayal of a character in a work of fiction in such a way that the reader or audience seems to learn more about them as they develop, change, and grow.

REAT GAMES STAND ON THE SHOULDERS OF THE good games that came before. For decades, Sony has been making very good *God of War* games. It's a celebrated franchise with a compelling and powerful hero at the helm. But there's no doubt that games like *Uncharted 4* and *The Last of Us* influenced the story told in Sony's latest *God of War* game. In a franchise steeped in outstanding below-the-neck action, Sony finally turned their focus inward and provided the character depth gamers have wanted since the franchise arrived on the scene in 2005.

God of War is a jaw-dropping spectacle, the result of the combined efforts of over two hundred talented developers, that lives up to the high expectation of a AAA published title. It is awe-inspiring that so many people can come together to make something fantastic in every way: from its visuals to the music to the gameplay design to the acting to the story, everything is on point and perfectly focused.

God of War wastes no time dropping gamers into a somber story. You play as Kratos, who is pretending to be something he's not—a mortal and a good father. He and his ten-year-old son, Atreus, are building a funeral pyre out of trees for his recently deceased wife. Kratos gently carries Faye's limp body, reverently wrapped in a funeral sack, to the wooden altar as Atreus lights it with a candle. They spend a moment sending her silent goodbyes before embarking on Faye's dying request to spread her ashes from the highest peak in Asgard.

God of War © Santa Monica Studios / Sony Entertainment Interactive LLC

This basic story has been told before, not just once, but time and time again. Unfortunately, a lot of people wrote this game off weeks before it even came out as a clone of *The Last of Us* because of Kratos and Atreus's parent-child relationship. But stories like these will continue to be told as long as there are parents and children, and children who one day will become parents. And that's not a bad thing. We need stories that can simulate high-stakes relationships like these, to warn us of pitfalls we may approach in real life and to teach us how to avoid or overcome them. *God of War* reminds us to not let our past define our future. To fearlessly expose our fears, weaknesses, and mistakes to our loved ones. We are shown that our actions as adults and parents will affect those who look up to us for guidance. And that being a role model can leave a lasting, positive—or sometimes, sadly, negative—imprint.

There is no denying the biological attraction we have to a story like *God of War*. When we watch Kratos hesitate to place a loving hand on his son's shoulder after they hunt a deer, it strikes something familiar in all of us. For some reason, Kratos, a literal god who has killed other gods and fearlessly battled terrifying monsters from other dimensions, shies away at the thought of showing affection to his son. We can't help but wonder why. And most of all, we want to know how these complex emotions get resolved for this rough, seemingly stoic man. It's obvious to see the outward struggles he faces, but to fully understand the machinations that Kratos wrestles with internally requires us to dive deep into his background, and how it applies to the way he feels about Atreus.

In the previous *God of War* games, set in Greek mythology, you also played as Kratos, who was driven primarily by base animal instincts of lust and survival. He made a deal with a god he should have refused, got his revenge, and became a god himself as well as becoming the Ghost of Sparta. A name he received for his pale white skin, a physical mark and permanent reminder of his gravest mistakes. The unique twist *God of War* for PS4 takes is to pit Kratos against a foe he is perhaps the least qualified to face: fatherhood. And the beautiful thing about this game is that you don't have to have played every game before it to enjoy it, because the conflict we crave centers on a new relationship between Kratos and Atreus.

One of the biggest takeaways from playing the story of *God of War* is how masterfully the creative team at Sony handled the character development of both Atreus and Kratos. First, we witness the lessons Kratos teaches his son, and then we see it unravel as those lessons come back to bite Kratos as Atreus exhibits his own behaviors in a terrifying way. But before we can get into this, it helps if we go back and learn more about Kratos. Sony knew this as well and were more than happy to take us there.

Kratos was deeply ashamed of his past and thought he ran away from it when he left Greece behind and settled in Midgard, a realm ruled by the gods of Norse mythology. He buried his iconic weapons, the Chaos Blades; hid the distinctive scars their chains seared into his forearms; and tried to start a new life as a mortal. He met a woman named Faye, and the two fell in love. He told her the secrets of his past and his true nature, but surprisingly, it didn't scare her off. They built a house and had a son.

Kratos tried to convince his subconscious self that he was leaving the past behind, but his greatest fears would return to haunt him. He couldn't escape the deeply sown resentment he has for the gods, and that includes himself.

Instead of dealing with the challenges of being a new father, Kratos often went away on protracted hunts while Faye lovingly raised Atreus and watched over the homestead. She told her son stories about the Norse gods and their mythology and taught him how to use a bow and hunt, how to read and speak the languages of the realms, but she never told him his father was a god. Atreus, often sick and bedridden, was raised as a mortal and forbidden to leave the forest that surrounded their home.

Then Atreus's mother died, and Kratos returned to help burn her body and raise his son. At the opening of the game, Atreus is confused. He's obviously devastated at losing his mother, and he's intimidated by his brooding father, a man he doesn't really know. Kratos wants to begin their journey to the tallest mountain in haste, so he tests Atreus's skills by leaving on a hunt while Faye's body cremates. As I played through this part of the game, I got the impression that Kratos was trying to connect with his son through something they both enjoy, hunting. His dialogue is gruff, but he seems dedicated to teaching Atreus. And although it was contrary to what I knew of Kratos in past games, it could even be interpreted as nurturing, which is not his normal nature.

Atreus is surprisingly adept at identifying animal tracks, which impresses Kratos right away. What disappoints him, however, is the child's overwhelming excitement when he catches a glimpse of their prey. Atreus fires an errant, misplaced shot at the buck, putting it on guard and making it harder to hunt. Kratos quickly and aggressively disciplines his son, barking at him for his folly. He also takes away Atreus's bow and orders him to follow the deer unarmed. This interaction sets the uneasy tone for their relationship.

Kratos is a Spartan who was trained since he was a boy to fight and survive. He was tested greatly, in horrible conditions by warriors stronger and better than him. For the first years of Atreus's life, Kratos avoided his son to try to spare him from his destiny. But now that he is forced to be there for him, the only thing he knows is to treat him like a soldier, which is a new dynamic for the emotionally tender Atreus.

God of War © Santa Monica Studios / Sony Entertainment Interactive LLC

Early on in the game, Atreus, in an attempt to please his father, responds often with "yes, sir" and apologizes frequently. But as the game continues, the two grow closer together, and he asks Kratos to teach him how to be more effective in battle. Atreus is smart and responds quickly to his commands. He even apologizes less often after Kratos tells him to stop.

When we read, play, or watch a story, we often have the advantage of knowing more about the story than the characters do. It's part of what makes stories so compelling, because we have that constant "oh, don't open that door. I know what's behind there" mindset that adds tension and surprise. As we watch Atreus move from being an innocent boy to a more independent version of himself, we start to see that the manner in which Kratos commands him around is causing him to start to rebel a bit from Kratos's strict and unforgiving behavior. It's a great use of a term called dramatic irony, when the player is aware before Kratos that his actions are affecting his son negatively.

Kratos's influence happens so gradually that it's hard to notice what's happening. It just feels natural. This first hunting expedition is a great example of this. As they track the deer, Kratos stops to rob a grave, and Atreus warns him of spirits that might seek vengeance. Faye taught her son to respect the dead and the old ways. Kratos's curt response is that they should "do what [they] please." They watch the deer slip into an old temple, a sacred, ruined structure Faye forbade Atreus from entering. Kratos defiantly hefts the massive stone doors apart and storms inside, daring whatever god that watches over the sanctuary to strike him down. Throughout their quest, Kratos tries to teach his son not to interfere with other people's business, no matter how innocent or helpless they may be. The only thing that matters to Kratos in the entire game is releasing Faye's ashes from the tallest peak in Midgard.

This aloof, rebellious attitude is important to keep in mind, because it comes back to play a part in Atreus's character development later in the game.

Atreus spies their prey about ten yards away through some branches. It's just far enough of a target for him to hit. He looks at his father, and Kratos hands him back his bow. Kratos kneels behind him to help. He instructs his son to take a deep breath, draw all the way to his chest, exhale, and fire. The arrow strikes true, and Atreus turns to his father and leaps in excitement. It's a tender moment. Perhaps the first between the two of them. They approach the dying animal, and Kratos guides his son to use Faye's knife to finish the job they started. Kratos looks out on the horizon over their trophy and notices his son watching him. Then Atreus copies him. Proud, Kratos lifts a hand behind Atreus's back, then hesitates. He pulls the knife out of the carcass and hands it to Atreus. The moment is spoiled when a gigantic blue hand stretches up from the cliff below and snatches their deer. The giant ogre, two stories tall, challenges the puny hunters.

This fight shows how *God of War* for PS4 is different from its predecessors. Not only is it a totally different style of game in terms of gameplay design, but the stakes are much higher. Before, Kratos could throw caution to the wind and sacrifice everything to win. Previous games often made the fights more intense by giving Kratos more enemies to fight at once or larger, more challenging foes, but here things feel more intense because you are worried, with Kratos, about Atreus's not being able to hold his own. And if Kratos dies, then the boy will have to fend for himself.

The two fell the monster, and Atreus loses his temper, whips out Faye's knife, and frantically slashes shallow cuts into the dead ogre's thick hide, screaming and shouting. After a while, his father grabs him by the shoulders to settle him down. Atreus sways from side to side, and his eyes nearly drift shut, overwhelmed by the thrill of adrenaline that was so suddenly produced by his tiny system. Kratos tells him he isn't ready for their journey yet, which upsets Atreus. They return home, disappointed, from what could have been a simple bonding moment.

When they arrive home, Atreus is defiant and believes he is ready to travel to the top of the mountain, but Kratos has not changed his mind. The fast-moving plot continues as a stranger knocks at their door. No one has ever visited their home before because of the magic that protects their land from unwanted eyes, and Kratos tells Atreus to hide in the cellar. Kratos warily creaks open the oak door and is greeted by a thin, shirtless man covered in blue tattoos. He does not introduce himself, but we later learn this is Baldur, a god and son of

Odin, the Allfather, and Freya, goddess of the Vanir. Baldur wants to pick a fight with Kratos. And, although he doesn't mention it at this point in the game, he has also been ordered by the Allfather to capture Atreus and bring him to Asgard. Kratos tells him to leave or he will get the fight he wants. This results in perhaps one of the greatest boss fights I have ever witnessed, and Sony's placing this within the first thirty minutes of gameplay was a masterful decision. Not only does it set the stage for showing us what is to come, it also lets us know that Kratos might have met his match. For the first time, Kratos has found a foe he can't defeat, and as the game moves on and he smashes gods and monsters the size of skyscrapers, it really puts this fight in perspective that he can't defeat a man smaller than him. Not to mention that the entire fight scene happens without a single camera cut; the action is perfectly paced, and the dialogue feels both gritty and over the top. Yeah, it left an impression on me for sure.

Baldur, despite being a powerful god who can never die and feels no pain, loses to our pale, bearded hero. As Kratos limps back to his house, exhausted from the prolonged duel, he whispers a plea to Faye. He knows Atreus isn't ready for their journey. Kratos doesn't think he is ready, either. He doesn't know if he can do it without her. But they have to leave. The spell that hid them from prying eyes is broken; it is no longer safe to stay. Kratos retrieves Atreus.

Atreus is anxious to leave, and he can't help but ask a million questions. He is a sheltered, curious child who was told fantastic stories by his mother. As they march between the tall trees, he can barely contain his joy as he leaves his forest for the first time in his life. Not only that, but he finally feels healthy. We don't know how long he had been bedridden for, but the problem is often on Kratos's mind.

Kratos isn't familiar with how to express his emotions and is often short with Atreus. Sometimes he won't answer Atreus's questions at all, and the tension is palpable. But Atreus isn't stupid. He can detect some kind of bubbling animosity beneath the surface of his father's silent demeanor. He just can't put his finger on why his father doesn't seem to like him. And it only hurts more that he is trying his hardest to make his father accept him. He can't help but be a kid, and this is his first taste of freedom. It's understandable when he makes mistakes that set them back on their journey, and Kratos has to work hard to keep his temper at bay. The irony is, in previous titles, he never had to exercise control over his emotions—in fact, part of what made him such a terrifying force was his ability to unleash untamed fury to win battles. In giving him Atreus, the writers make us see this character, who's traditionally violent, in a new light.

As they travel on their long journey, Kratos warns Atreus to push away his emotions as well. But Atreus sees the hypocrisy in what his father demands. He can see Kratos struggle with his short temper, a trait the boy inherited from his godly father. Atreus doesn't understand why he should try to control himself, when his father uses his anger in battle all the time. Kratos tries to explain to the boy that he is not wise enough to know *how* to use his anger yet. But that is not something a young person wants to hear, no matter how true it may be.

Because of his decades of experience in warfare, Kratos knows where their path will take them. He warns his son that there will come a time when he has to kill and that he needs to shut his heart to others or the consequences can be painful. When Atreus inevitably kills his first human in self-defense, it is a second tender, yet haunting, moment between the two, reminiscent of the deer hunt. But instead of Atreus's excitement over killing the deer, he is deeply disturbed by what he had to do to survive. Kratos reminds him to close his heart.

This moment is one any child-father relationship can relate to. Kratos is trying to ease his son's pain and be a good father, but really, this becomes a major turning point in the development of Atreus. He behaves strangely immediately after, moving slowly, trying to comprehend it, but the weight is too much for the boy to handle. Kratos snaps him out of his stupor by telling him if he can't handle it, they will just return home. Atreus, who more than anything wants to prove he is mature, shakes the moment off once and for all.

It's a rare thing when a violent video game spends time showing how a person copes with killing another human being. And I tip my hat to the developers of *God of War* for prioritizing this important moment.

For whatever their reasons, the Norse gods continue to interfere with Atreus and Kratos's journey to the mountain. Thor's sons, Magni and Modi, on an errand for their father, confront them. The oafish brothers bully Atreus by calling his mother names and making fun of his scar. Kratos tries to warn his son to keep his cool, but it's too much for the juvenile firebrand to handle. He abandons his father and recklessly charges after Modi with a knife, who easily snatches up the child. Kratos, in his anger, kills Magni, cleaving his face with his Bifrost axe. Modi, stunned that his brother, a lesser Aesir god, has actually died, drops Atreus and scrambles back to Asgard in fear.

Kratos and Atreus think they are finally free of the gods' interruptions, but much later in the game, Modi returns. He shocks

Kratos motionless with his mace using the lightning powers he inherited from Thor and antagonizes Atreus again, making fun of his mother. Atreus loses his temper yet again and attacks, summoning a godlike power similar to Kratos's. But instead of unshackling his power from a well of divine potential, he short-circuits and passes out. Modi laughs at the poor boy's misfortune, which provokes his father. Slowly, Kratos breaks free of the lightning by grabbing Modi's elemental mace with his bare hands and tossing it aside. Modi runs away screaming again. Kratos picks up his son and takes him to Freya, Odin's ex-wife and master of the old ways, who might know of a way to cure him. And this is where we learn about the source of Atreus's malady.

Freya telling Kratos how to save Atreus in God of War © Santa Monica Studios / Sony Entertainment Interactive LLC

Freya instructs Kratos to travel to Hel, a frozen wasteland, carve out the heart of a monster that guides spirits to the afterlife, and bring it back to her. She tells him this will heal Atreus, but it will only stop the sickness. To cure the disease for good, Kratos must tell Atreus the truth, that he is also a god. At this point, we get a clear picture of two things: One, Atreus's sickness is caused by his mortal body struggling with the unknown godly powers and potential within him. And two, we now understand Kratos's great internal conflict. For multiple games in the franchise, we've been hearing how Kratos hates the gods, all of them, even himself. He's known all along that Atreus was a god, and he is torn because of his lifelong disdain of the very thing his son has become.

And to add more layers to this story, we learn that Baldur, the god that fought and lost to Kratos at the beginning of the game, is Freya's son, and that she, too, has failed as a parent. Out of fear, Freya selfishly gave him what she thought was a blessing. She wished he would never feel pain and never die. But Baldur resents her for what she's done, because not only can he not feel pain, he can't feel anything. He can't taste, he can't feel the temperature in the room, not even the wind on his face. A truly terrible curse. Freya tells Kratos not to make the same mistakes she did by hiding the truth from Atreus. And after her encouragement, Kratos promises to swallow his pride and do the right thing for his son. To survive Hel, Kratos needs the fiery power of his Chaos Blades, weapons he thought he had left behind forever with the past he had escaped. But for his son, he uses them again, retrieving the heart for Freya, who cures Atreus.

After thanking Freya, Kratos tells Atreus he is cursed because he is a god. He explains to his son that he kept it a secret because he wanted to spare him the lifetime of tragedy and anguish he has experienced. Atreus knows his father hates the gods, and now he finally feels as though he has an answer for his father's strange antipathy toward him. But he doesn't understand *why* Kratos hates the gods.

Atreus likes the idea of being a god, and after learning he's immortal, he becomes boastful and full of himself. In his youthful foolishness, Atreus thinks he is a better god than Odin and the other Aesir, because he is his father's son. Kratos is his hero, and he emulates him in almost everything he does, including the two formative lessons about doing as you please and closing your heart to other people. The subtle changes we've seen in Atreus to this point are now left behind. Now the lives of mortals have less meaning.

Atreus feels he is a god worthy enough to judge for himself who should live or die. Little actions, like Kratos's hesitating to place a hand on his son's back after killing the deer, take on new meaning. Now when Kratos tries to support his son with a hand, Atreus steps away because he feels as though he doesn't need anyone. He is no longer the meek, sickly, sheltered lamb. Now he is a god who finally has power. And no one can tell him what to do, including Kratos.

This is when the internal conflict is at its greatest. Kratos faces giants, trolls, dragons, and imminent mortal threats without fear. Challenges that would be terrifying for most people. But the things regular people face on a daily basis are what really scare him. He has no experience with how to build a healthy relationship with your child. And worse, Atreus is no longer just a child. Kratos is raising a god who acts with impunity based on whims. How are you supposed to tell a god they're wrong?

Atreus reaches a tipping point when Modi appears a final time, bloody and blue, on their way to the mountain peak. Thor had beaten his son half to death for letting Magni die. Kratos, seeing that he is already beaten, tells Atreus they should let him live. But Atreus doesn't agree. "He should pay for what he said about Mother. After all, we're gods. And we can do whatever. We. Want." The once curious and playful child whips out his knife and stabs Modi in the throat. Kratos, utterly furious, tries to reprimand his son, but Atreus has transformed. He flippantly ignores his father's scalding rebukes, which at one point worked like a charm. Atreus doesn't feel an ounce of guilt for what he has done. Quite the change from the helpless whelp who cried over the death of a stranger who was trying to murder him.

Kratos doesn't know what to say. What can he say? He taught Atreus how to kill. He taught him to close his heart to his enemies. He taught him to do as he pleased. Every lesson Kratos taught Atreus, directly or indirectly, has come back to haunt him.

They continue to make their way up the mountain, but Atreus has stopped obeying Kratos's commands. He doesn't wait for the player to initiate a fight before going into combat anymore. He is like an uncontrollable fiend. They make it to the peak but are interrupted again, by Baldur, who agitates Atreus by insulting his mother again. Kratos forcefully throws his son back but is stopped in his tracks when Atreus shoots Kratos with a shock arrow. That's right. Atreus has changed so much that he's willing to harm his father, who has been his lifeline, because of his newly discovered conceit. Stunned (literally), Kratos watches hopelessly as Atreus runs at Baldur with his mother's knife drawn. Baldur easily sweeps the boy off his feet and leaps off the mountain with Atreus in his arms. Kratos, abandoning all sense of self-preservation, revives himself and jumps off after them.

Falling blindly, Kratos peers through the mist as a giant dragon comes into view hundreds of feet below him. He lands heavily on the beast's tail and climbs up to where Baldur is sitting at the base of the neck. They brawl over Atreus's unconscious body, and the dragon flies through a dimension gate back to Hel. And if that isn't the most *God of War* sentence I've ever written, I don't know what is. Kratos gains the upper hand as they are flying and tears his boy out of Baldur's arms. Separating from their foe, they crash-land in the spiritual dimension. Then Atreus regains consciousness. Kratos doesn't know if reprimanding his errant son will work, but he doesn't care. He doesn't want the fact to be lost on Atreus that he is solely responsible for damning them to Hel for what might be eternity. Atreus, dejected, acts as if he might have finally learned his lesson.

God of War © Santa Monica Studios / Sony Entertainment Interactive LLC

They find themselves trapped in a dimension that forces you to relive your greatest mistakes, regrets, and fears forever. From a distance, they spot Baldur pacing anxiously around his own ghost and the ghost of his mother. Fascinated, the silent pair watch the god, driven mad by his gift of invulnerability, spit encouragement at his past self to kill Freya as she informs him of the blessing she's given him. But these images are like holograms, recordings of the past, and spirit Baldur doesn't listen. The apparition describes to Freya the pain of being invulnerable and leaves her be. What spirit Baldur doesn't understand is that it is her love for him that actually caused his invulnerability. It was part of the curse from the start. The real Baldur screams at himself to go back and strangle her, but it's useless. His cries echo through the misty wasteland. He falls to his knees and sobs uncontrollably into his lap, cursing himself for being such a coward.

Kratos and Atreus finally escape Hel, and somehow, so does Baldur, who will stop at nothing to fulfill his father's command. Surprisingly, when they return to the realm of the living, Freya is there. She was inspired by Kratos's honesty to Atreus and wants to finally make amends with her son. But, after seeing Baldur in Hel, Kratos and Atreus know nothing will persuade him to forgive her. The estranged mother and son have not seen each other for hundreds of years, and Baldur's seething hatred for her has only multiplied in that time.

When Baldur sees Freya, he becomes so blind with fury he forgets all about his quest. Freya apologizes to her son, but there is simply no point in even trying. Baldur grinds his teeth, bares his fists, and walks toward the goddess. And this is where we see a major development in Kratos's character. The old Kratos would have taken advantage of Baldur's distraction and spirited his son away, taking Faye's ashes to the tallest peak in Midgard, finally uninterrupted. Instead, Kratos commits to being a better god. To protecting people, even if you gain nothing from it. Worse, interfering with Baldur and Freya's conflict puts himself and his son's life at risk. But he does it to set an example for his son. Kratos's path has been wrought with vengeance, parents killing children, and children killing parents, and he loves Atreus too much to continue that pattern for him. Someone has to do the right thing, and it has to start somewhere. Finally, Kratos comes full circle.

First, he tries to convince Baldur that vengeance won't give him peace, but the other god won't listen. Baldur will stop at nothing to kill Freya, even if it means having to go through Kratos. Atreus, who has also come full circle, puts his ego aside and works together with his father to protect Freya from Baldur. The fearsome invulnerable god, now fueled with passionate vengeance, fights back twice as hard as before. Baldur isn't going to change his mind. He's been driven insane by not being able to feel, and he laments how he can't even kill himself to end the madness.

Eventually, Baldur attacks Atreus, and they discover Baldur's one true weakness, mistletoe. It's a strange rule pulled directly from Norse mythology. At first, it felt almost arbitrary, but that fits well with the type of Vanir magic Freya performs. The spell is broken, which means that he can feel again and that he can die. Yet Baldur insists they continue to battle, because it feels so good to feel again.

Throughout the battle sequence, Freya tries to stop the fight because she still thinks she can persuade her son to forgive her. Now that she's been given the chance to talk to him, she accepts whatever fate he chooses for her. Even if it means she dies by his hands. But Kratos intervenes again and snaps his neck. Finally, Baldur dies.

Freya is distraught beyond belief at the death of her beloved son. Kratos tells her Baldur brought it upon himself, but she won't accept that it was the right thing to do. They leave Freya, who issues a very colorful threat to murder Kratos if she ever sees him again.

Their quest is nearing an end as the two walk from Midgard to their final destination. Kratos faces his greatest fear by telling his son everything about his past. How he killed his father, Zeus, and killed many deserving and undeserving people. Atreus is distraught because he doesn't want his life to be like his father's. He doesn't want it to end as it did for Baldur and Freya. Kratos commits to Atreus to be a better god, and they promise to grow together. They will be the gods they choose to be, for the right reasons. They must be better.

After all their hard work, at last they make it to the mountain peak undisturbed. Kratos finally places a hand behind his son's back and hands him Faye's ashes. Then Kratos unwraps the bandages hiding his scars and confesses he has nothing left to hide.

The game, although a harrowing journey, ends on a moment of hope. There's unspoken harmony between the two of them as we get the impression that Atreus can offer something to Kratos no one—not even Kratos himself—has ever been able to give. An opportunity to forgive himself and move on.

BOOK REPORT:

Horizon Zero Dawn

Horizon Zero Dawn © Guerrilla Games / Sony Interactive Entertainment

INITIAL RELEASE DATE AND PLATFORM:

February 2017 for PlayStation 4

WHERE ELSE CAN IT BE FOUND?

In August 2020, Guerrilla Games released a Windows PC build.

CATEGORY:

Linear Narrative, Third-Person Sci-Fi Shooter

MAIN CHARACTERS:

Aloy, the strong and willful protagonist. She is the only playable character in the game, a Nora Brave, a Seeker, and machine hunter of unparalleled skill.

Rost, the closest thing to a father Aloy will ever know. He raised her from infancy, trained her, and protected her.

Dr. Elisabet Sobeck, a scientist who passed away over a thousand years ago.

SETTING:

There are so many unique and interesting characters as you explore the world of *Horizon Zero Dawn* that it would take a few pages to begin to list them. In this apocalyptic world filled with dangerous semiorganic robots and perhaps even more dangerous cults, you can't help but feel in constant peril as you fight for survival in a beautifully concepted environment filled with colorful trees, formidable mountains, and terrifyingly open plains of waving grass.

STORY SUMMARY:

The game opens with Aloy, an orphaned warrior coming of age in a time when dino-size machines reminiscent of birds, mammals, and insects roam and rule the earth. But the story of her fantastic world, we soon find out, began thousands of years ago. As Aloy fights the metal beasts and warring social groups and cults, she uncovers a past that is both shocking, yet oddly familiar, and terrifying.

Not only is Aloy the best hope for humanity today, but she also learns that she (or a version of her) was once, over a thousand years ago, the savior of an earth nearly stripped of all life.

In a story that combines the mystery of cults, the science of cloning and DNA manipulation, the hunger of megaton creatures, and the grace of a powerful warrior with a worthy quest, we get to question our humanity, our responsibility for the world we live in today, and perhaps even our morality.

WHAT DID YOU THINK OF THIS STORY?

This game has real weight. It packs a message of what might happen if science is left unregulated and the overwhelming cost of what humans can do to a planet if left to their own devices. The game points out our ability to both improve and destroy the things we hold dear when they are in our hands. It's the kind of story that lingers for years as you see small reminders of what might be held in store for all of us.

But all that heavy stuff aside, the game is freaking fun. The scale of the metal and bone beasts in this world is outstanding, and you are filled with a real sense of power when you craft an arrow and launch it as the final blow into a robotic creature with the size and attitude of a Tyrannosaurus rex.

Add some of the best voice acting and animation that technology allows today and this game is simply a winner. Who could ask for more?

Story
Structures

Cliché. Formulaic. Predictable. Not words you usually associate with greatness, right? I mean, don't we all prefer innovative, original, and unique?

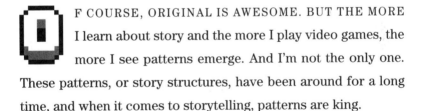 F COURSE, ORIGINAL IS AWESOME. BUT THE MORE I learn about story and the more I play video games, the more I see patterns emerge. And I'm not the only one. These patterns, or story structures, have been around for a long time, and when it comes to storytelling, patterns are king.

A good place to start looking into this is the three-act structure. Writers either swear *by* it or swear *at* it. At its core, there are only three steps. The setup, the confrontation, and the resolution. And while one of the biggest complaints about this structure is that it can be predictable, from a writing perspective, nothing could be further from the truth. The intent of this structure is quite simply to keep the beginning, the middle, and ending of your story separated.

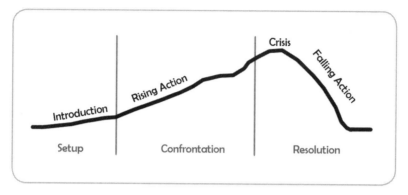

Usually when people refer to this structure, this is the model that is used. A great example of act 1 (the setup) in games can be found in Bethesda's *The Elder Scrolls* series. In *Skyrim*, the player character is dropped into an execution scene and forced to make immediate decisions with almost no backstory. Bethesda didn't do this by accident. They wanted the player to get to know the main character, which can be tricky when a game lets you design your own protagonist in an epic, hundred-hour story.

Up to this point, most of the modifications you've made to your player character are visual. And while those visuals help us bond to the character, they do little to tell us who the character is or how they act. So Bethesda forces the player to make a powerful early gameplay choice that helps the gamer craft a backstory based on their decisions that will start to define who they are in the game.

It's brilliant, and something unique to games, but at the same time it feels familiar. After all, we don't usually know much about the main character when we begin reading a novel or watching a film. We form opinions during the setup and introduction. Much of *Skyrim*'s act 1 is spent exploring. This game is an open-world experience that lets you roam at your own pace. You discover, converse with NPC characters, and learn the environment, which

Bethesda has stuffed with loads of lore and backstory. But Bethesda also guides you into some dramatic scenes early on that will continue to help you define who your character really is based on your in-game decisions.

And *Skyrim* doesn't let you hang around forever in this discovery stage. You get some time to flesh out the world and define what your character looks and acts like, then *blamo*, just like that, you meet the antagonist and the action rises. Which leads us to act 2.

Generally, in video games, the second act is a bit trickier. Part of this is because of the power of player choice and how allowing gamers the ability to affect the outcome of the story can mess with things from a writing perspective.

It's becoming increasingly rare to find a single-player-focused game where you don't have options that will, to one degree or another, alter the outcome of the story. Act 2 is usually the longest part of any story and is often written with the antagonist in mind. Even if you never see the antagonist doing any planning during act 2, almost every obstacle the protagonist will face comes about because the antagonist wants to win and force the hero to lose. This has been true since before Donkey Kong first threw flaming barrels at Mario.

In act 2, you can usually expect some form of game changer that comes out of left field to screw up the protagonist's plans. It could be something like the loss of a key ally, whether a perceived loss, such as Sully's getting shot in the first *Uncharted*, or the actual death of Yusuf Tazim in *Assassin's Creed: Revelations*. You may even encounter a point of initial failure, where the protagonist must retrain or reexamine a choice to overcome that failure before they get to act 3.

Often, one of these can lead to a low point for the protagonist, known as the long dark night of the soul. It's that moment when all seems lost for our hero. When compounded with cleverly increased difficulty in gameplay, this can be especially challenging. I'd guess that more controllers are thrown during this time in a game's story than any other. Or maybe that's just me.

This dramatic rise in action, this increase in internal conflict and external struggle, is when a good story throws us into a crisis. We hit the climax of the conflict and enter act 3.

As with any good story, the final battle will likely take place on the antagonist's turf, putting the protagonist at a significant disadvantage. This is demonstrated when the Spartans and Marines assault the Flood vessel in *Halo*, or when Batman finally infiltrates the asylum and meets with the Joker in *Batman: Arkham Asylum*.

It will usually be broken into two separate stages in the game. Stage one will be the big assault just to get to the antagonist, as in the first *Mass Effect*, when you work your way to the Council's chambers on the Citadel to fight Saren. Stage two is, of course, the ultimate boss battle itself. How you get your hero out of trouble will depend largely on your skill in that battle. Will you spring upon the bad guy and save the day or plummet and die, letting down those that count on you most?

Okay, I know there are a lot of references going on here, but I'm hoping you'll begin to see how powerful this story structure can be. I also hope you'll begin to see the diverse potential that a structure like this can provide. You can compare the underlying structure of *Grim Fandango* and *Halo*, but nobody would confuse the two from a story, plot, or character standpoint.

God of War is a good example of Freytag's Pyramid, another popular story structure. There are some subtle differences between the three-act structure and Freytag's method for crafting a story. Calling out the inciting incident at the end of the exposition phase is one, but probably more obvious is the use of the denouement (day-new-mah) after the major conflict has been resolved.

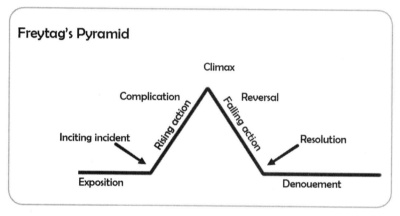

The graph above works well for showing the elements of the story structure, but it's pretty far off as far as time spent in the game or story itself. If we were to map this graph along a typical story time line, the graph would look more like this:

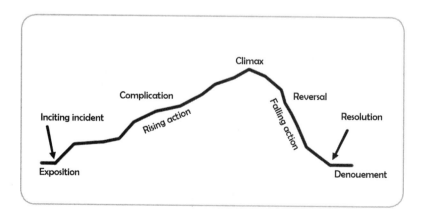

Another thing the original graph doesn't show well is weight. Story weight. Importance. If you think of each step along the way as changing the momentum or direction of the plot and creating big moments in the story, then this second graph is probably more accurate. It also shows that the bulk of the time spent in the story is during that long struggle period. Building and resolving conflict.

We could go through and map each point of *God of War* against this graph, but that is probably best saved for another book/blog post/podcast. But I think it's worth pointing out three quick things here. Some of the exposition and world-building of *God of War* takes place in previous games. If you've played the series, then you know that Kratos has a heck of a reputation. However, his change in character is obvious as you start the game and find out that he's a father and that he's trying to leave his past behind him. The inciting incident happens when he is set on a journey, with his son, to scatter the ashes of Faye from the highest mountain. Basically, the inciting incident happens in the first thirty seconds of the game. That's kind of a big risk for a developer to take on, but for me, it paid off.

And other major thing that removes *God of War* from the three-act structure and puts it into this Freytag's Pyramid camp is how Sony uses the denouement (a French word which loosely means "the end of things," or "untying") to show us that this game truly is a tragedy. I won't spoil it here, but the last chunk of the game, after the "big boss fight" is heartbreaking and beautifully handled.

If you play through the game, watch for these elements and see how Sony uses this structure to deliver such a punch.

But probably the most commonly used dramatic structure in story-telling today is the hero's journey. Examples of this structure abound in modern media, from *Star Wars: A New Hope* to *Luigi's Mansion 3* to *The Lion King*. It works because it sends us on a predictable journey from the call to begin an adventure, along a struggle-filled path, to a return with new perspective and character growth.

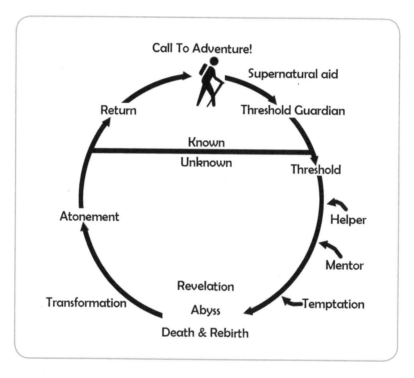

While this structure has been around for centuries, it was in 1949 that author Joseph Campbell theorized that humans can't help but fall into the same patterns when telling stories about their heroes. Campbell is widely credited with being the one to point this out and add definition to the hero's journey in his book *The Hero with a Thousand Faces*. The crux of his argument was that nearly all of humankind's myths, stories, and religions are based on the same universal and eternal concepts and that the heroes that drive them more or less follow the same basic steps.

While there are different definitions and levels of detail for the hero's journey, ranging from seventeen discrete steps down to as low as four, I'm going to take a quick stab at pointing out what I think are the most important steps within this structure. The six steps are as follows. And yes, I'm using one of my all-time faves to show the way.

THE LEGEND OF ZELDA: OCARINA OF TIME

Step 1: Call to Adventure, Part 1: The Call

Link, living in a small, idyllic village away from the hustle and bustle of the world, is awakened by Navi, who summons him to the Great Deku Tree. Link goes to the tree as requested and is tasked with ending the curse placed on him by Ganondorf. He is then told to take the Kokiri Emerald to Princess Zelda in Hyrule Castle.

The Legend of Zelda: Ocarina of Time © Nintendo

Step 2: Call to Adventure, Part 2: Loss

Link loses the guardian spirit of his forest, the Great Deku Tree. This loss is particularly hard on the young hero given his valiant efforts to save the spirit by ending the curse within him. And as expected, the effects of this loss are seen as soon as Link returns to the Kokiri village. Mido scolds him as he walks out, and the rest of the Kokiri all watch Link with concern. A balance has been shaken.

The Legend of Zelda: Ocarina of Time © Nintendo

Step 3: The Threshold

In this stage, the hero almost always encounters a person who expands their initial errand. In *Ocarina of Time*, Link delivers the Kokiri Emerald to Zelda, who then explains her vision and distrust of Ganondorf to Link and asks him to collect the remaining two Spiritual Stones. Suddenly, Link's errand has expanded into an adventure that will take him all throughout the land of Hyrule.

STEP 4: Challenges and Temptations

Considering Nintendo's E-rated reputation, many of the conventional ideas of temptations don't exactly occur in the Zelda series. Typically, temptations refer to external influences that try to lure the hero from their path, and since the Zelda series is typically very focused plotwise, there are rarely if ever significant temptations that Link faces. Challenges, however, play right into the series' style.

In *Ocarina of Time*, Link gathers the remaining two Spiritual Stones by ending the curses Ganondorf placed on Dodongo's Cavern and Lord Jabu-Jabu. In addition to this, Link completes several tasks for the Gorons and the Zora before gaining the ability or permission to enter the dungeons. It's a large section of the plot where development comes slowly, and most of what is seen is setup for later revelations—as it should be.

The Legend of Zelda: Ocarina of Time © Nintendo

Step 5a: The Abyss (Death and Return)

The abyss does not necessarily mean literal death—Link doesn't actually die in any of the games to date, after all—but rather a symbolic death, followed by an equally symbolic rebirth, usually accompanied with the acquisition of new abilities. In the *Legend of Zelda* series overall, the abyss is usually a critical oversight in Link's plans that allows the villain to gain the upper hand, if only temporarily, and maneuver themselves into a position of greater power.

In *Ocarina of Time* specifically, this occurs when Link returns the Spiritual Stones to Zelda. Before he can get to the castle gates, Zelda and Impa run by on horseback, tossing the Ocarina of Time behind them, just as Ganondorf steps out and taunts Link. While returning the Stones to the Temple of Time, Link opens the Door of Time and draws the Master Sword, which allows Ganondorf access to the Sacred Realm and the Triforce. When Link emerges seven years later, the world outside has taken on a dark and foreboding appearance, a fairly direct symbol of the idea of passing through the underworld.

Step 5b: Transformation and Atonement

Before moving on, one more aspect of the abyss needs to be discussed. The symbolic death, even though followed with a symbolic rebirth, leaves a lasting mark for which the hero must atone. Since Link's symbolic death in each of the three games is a result of an unforeseeable, but still critical, error in judgment, these losses are on his hands and he must atone for them. In *Ocarina of Time*, this mark is the corruption of the Sacred Realm and the splitting of the Triforce.

Link's atonement in *Ocarina of Time* is the awakening of the sages. As a result of Ganondorf's newfound powers, the temples scattered around Hyrule that would awaken the sages in their time of need are cursed. Link travels to the Forest, Fire, Water, Shadow, and Spirit Temples, awakening the five sages (Rauru, the sixth, was already awakened in the Temple of Light) and gaining the six Spirit Medallions. With the six sages awakened, Ganondorf can be defeated.

STEP 6: THE RETURN

The return for this game happens when Ganondorf is defeated. Actually, this is the return for quite a few of the Zelda games. Ganondorf just can't take the hint.

It usually happens at the end of a long and difficult journey, and in *Ocarina of Time*, Link has aged a lifetime in seven years. So, even though Zelda returns him to his own time, as things were at the beginning of the game, it does not last. Link, changed forever by the events of the game, goes off in search of Navi, leading to the events of *Majora's Mask*, which is a wonderful way to tease the story along for a future game.

The Legend of Zelda: Ocarina of Time © Nintendo

The trials of his adventure have left an indelible mark upon him, an unending thirst for adventure, and an inability to return to the way things once were. And isn't that the very core of *The Legend of Zelda*? There is always another story to be told, even if it's the same one that has been told several times before. The true legend of Zelda is the hero's journey—a boy in green, facing impossible odds, conquering these odds, and moving on to another adventure, another day.

BOOK REPORT:

Hades

Hades © Supergiant Games

INITIAL RELEASE DATE AND PLATFORM:

September 2020 for PC and Nintendo Switch

WHERE ELSE CAN IT BE FOUND?

This game was a powerhouse on PC and Switch, so it isn't surprising to see that since its launch it's made its way to the PS4, PS5, Xbox One, and the Xbox Series X/S.

Fun Fact:

This game cleaned up in the Tenth Annual New York Game Awards. It won in the game of the year, best music, best writing, and best acting categories.

Category:

Branching Narrative, Rogue-like, Action Dungeon Crawler

Main Characters:

Zagreus, the strong son of Hades

Hades, the lord of the Underworld

The Olympians, a whole cast of fun and memorable Greek gods, make an appearance along with residents of the Underworld such as Sisyphus, Eurydice, and Patroclus.

Setting:

The game is presented in a third-person, isometric view, which allows for wonderful arcade action and beautiful, colorful lighting. It takes place in the Underworld in four major "biomes," or locales: Tartarus (dark, eerie green lights flood stone paths and dangerous ballrooms), Asphodel (black and orange, filled with lava and floating islands of brimstone), Elysium (emerald pools, shafts of light, and open meadows filled with deadly enemies), and the Temple of Styx (earthy browns and blue, pillars of stone, and cobblestone paths).

Story Summary:

Filled with characters and story from Greek myths, *Hades* is a visually stunning game with slick controls. And while the gameplay is the thing that pulled me to this game at first, it was the story

Supergiant Games added to the mechanics that turned this into one of the most addicting story games of the year.

Warning. You're going to die in this game. A lot. Like, maybe even more than in other rogue-likes. Adding random encounters to an already mechanically challenging game can make it nearly impossible at times. Supergiant didn't stray away from this; in fact, they made it the core of their story. You play Zagreus, the rebellious heartthrob son of Hades who is hell-bent on getting out of hell. Hades offers him the chance, but he must fight his way out to make that happen. And as I said, you die. A lot. And when you do, Zag respawns back at home in a pool of blood to try again. And again.

What Did You Think of This Story?

In a rogue-like game, players start with nothing and battle their way through random encounters, with random weapons and random abilities. The excitement comes from the never-ending replay ability, and in seeing how far you can get before dying, then starting over again. How can you add a story to a game that rolls the dice like that?

Well, the dazzling team at Supergiant Games cracked this nut with *Hades*, a rogue-like dungeon crawler. This gameplay is full of plot, because, unlike most traditional rogue-likes, you don't lose everything upon dying. There are a few items that you keep, making each attempt at escaping hell a bit easier as you build Zagreus's skill tree. These things were all granted to you by other gods—uncles, aunts, and cousins—each willing to get back at Hades in their own way by aiding his son on his quest to get the hell out of hell.

And that's not all that carries over. The NPCs you interact with remember your journey as well. These characters will comment on your progress with some witty dialogue, making you feel as though they are also invested in your journey. And let me tell you, there is a *ton* of dialogue here. Every time I die, I expect that I've heard the last of the new dialogue, but the game continues to surprise me with more.

In the end, while I love Zag, it was the antagonist that filled me with determination to beat the game. Hades, who is definitely not father of the year, takes turns rebuking you for your failure and mocking your attempts at escaping the hellish dungeon he's created, seemingly to ruin your life. Literally. And for what? What does he have to lose if you escape?

Well, I'm going to leave that part up to you to discover. This game is hard, but the challenge is half the fun. Filled with the brightest, most exciting cast of characters and adversaries you could ever hope for. It's a perfect example of using gameplay and game mechanics, like dying, to twist the internal conflict knife so artfully as it sticks in your back. The way that Supergiant Games surrounds this arcade, rogue-like game with a compelling story that you just can't quit makes going to hell a whole lot more enjoyable.

Undertale

Juxtaposition (N.)

The act or instance of placing two or more characters, things, or concepts side by side to compare, contrast, or create a display of their profound differences.

AKING A NARRATIVE ROLE-PLAYING GAME IS A challenging endeavor. You're going up against some of the greatest story games ever made and trying to prove that you belong. *Undertale* is a profoundly personal game to me and absolutely deserves a place in the hall of interactive storytelling fame. And not just because it spoke to me on an emotional level and taught me about morality. But also because of what it says about tropes of its genre and video games in general, and how it takes advantage of its medium to say those things. On top of all that, it's fun to play, has a great story, and is one of the funniest games I've ever played.

Before I get into it, I have to give you a specific spoiler warning. *Undertale* is best to experience going in blind because it has a lot of fantastic twists. So, if you haven't played it yet and still want to, I recommend you do that before reading this chapter.

What's amazing is that *Undertale* was made by a very small team: writer, musician, and creator Toby Fox and artist Temmie Chang. And I don't think it could have been made any other way. Toby Fox grew up playing *EarthBound*, a wonderful, goofy cult classic from 1994, and its influence on *Undertale* is obvious. Both worlds are mysterious and humorous, the characters are likable (the main character is even wearing a striped shirt just like Ness, a character in *EarthBound*), and the story is engaging. *Undertale* is also reminiscent of *Shin Megami Tensei*, a monster-recruitment game that inspired *Pokémon* and was made by the same people who later made the *Persona* games. But what Fox felt was missing from most RPGs was *meaning* behind the gameplay. In that genre, you generally fight waves of faceless enemies, and the main characters seem to take no time to show that the massive loss of life has any effect on them whatsoever. Fox is quoted as saying: "They attack you, you heal; you attack them, they die. There's no meaning to that." From the very beginning, *Undertale* promises you can beat the game without killing a single enemy. This is called the pacifist route, the mechanic that allows the gameplay to have meaning.

Undertale © Toby Fox

In a game obviously influenced by classic JRPGs (Japanese role-playing games), this promise seems impossible. The bulk of JRPG gameplay has relied nearly exclusively on killing loads of enemies, monster or human, to harvest XP to upgrade your character. When Toby Fox announced the game on a crowd-funding platform and shared a playable demo of what to expect, longtime JRPG fans were pleasantly surprised at this twist and couldn't wait for more. The game climbed to over fifty times its funding goal, proving there was an enormous amount of interest in how a topsy-turvy RPG could be played without violence, but I don't think anyone was entirely prepared for what was in store.

If we agree that plot in video games can also be gameplay (running, jumping, slashing, puzzle-solving, etc.), then it makes sense that adding meaning to these actions would increase the power of the player's decisions. To me, the key word in Toby's quote above is *meaning*. Plot is better if it is meaningful to the characters and we can feel their reactions. The major thrust of *Undertale*'s gameplay is similar to most RPGs. It's a turn-based system where you, playing as the main character, engage in battle with enemies and have a list of actions you can take when it's your turn. With every enemy you face, you have the choice of whether to slay them, which is the traditional method of resolving conflict established by RPGs, or to spare them, which is the mechanic that sets the game apart. This also means that depending on the choices the player makes, the game can result in one of multiple endings, making it a linear branching game. There are three endings in *Undertale*: the neutral route, the genocide route, and the true pacifist route. (You get the genocide route by slaying every possible character, the pacifist route by sparing every possible character, and the neutral route by mixing both.)

But just because you *can* beat *Undertale* without killing a single enemy doesn't mean it's easy. In fact, it's the exact opposite—the true pacifist route is the most challenging to complete. Some enemies want to kill you very, very badly to get what they want. And this is part of where Fox's commentary on video games comes into play, because it's how he makes your choices feel like they matter. What he's saying is that it should be emotionally difficult to kill monsters in video games, not just strategically or mechanically.

Undertale makes it feel frustrating (in a good way) when you want to spare an enemy who will stop at nothing to kill you, even when killing that enemy would be easier. It makes you question what your reasons are for sparing every monster you see, if your goal is to just beat the game, when it would be objectively easier and faster to kill every enemy in your path.

The simple brilliance of *Undertale*'s design is the effects your choices have on your character, the world, and the monsters that live in it. Most people who play *Undertale*, including me, don't just want to beat the game, they want a fun yet challenging experience and a satisfying conclusion. It's how effortlessly *Undertale* walks this line that makes it so good.

Another thing *Undertale* does exceptionally well is use the silent protagonist to give decisions more impact. Unlike *Red Dead Redemption II*, *The Last of Us*, and *Uncharted*, where the gamer feels as though they are role playing *as* another character, Toby Fox wanted the player to feel as though they were playing as *themselves*. Fox believes the more personality you add to the protagonist, the harder it is to get absorbed into that role. So, in

Undertale, you play a mute, agender character with a couple of pixels for eyes and a straight line for a mouth. The game even looks eight-bit by design. Fox has stated that even if he had a team with nearly unlimited resources to make the game, he wouldn't change the art direction, because players will fill in missing visual details with their own imagination. As you play, you don't even question that you don't know the main character's name. In fact, it doesn't even come up until the end of the true pacifist route of the game. But for our purposes, so we can follow along with the story, I'm going to spoil the name here. The name of the protagonist in *Undertale* is Frisk.

The game begins when Frisk wakes up in the bottom of a cave. A yellow talking flower who introduces himself as Flowey notices Frisk is a human and doesn't belong in the Underground with the other monsters. To help Frisk, Flowey tells them to collect LV, an abbreviation for LOVE, in order to return home. Flowey instructs the player that if they collect enough "friendliness pellets," then their soul will become strong enough to return home. Flowey summons white sparkling lights around Frisk, and as Frisk reaches for them, they strike, dealing nineteen damage. Leaving Frisk on the brink of death, with just one hit point remaining. Flowey's smiley face transforms into something from a nightmare, and he laughs wickedly at Frisk's naivete. Flowey then states, in his commanding way, "In this world, it's kill or be killed." Then the demented flower summons the white projectiles again and threatens to kill Frisk to grow *his* soul.

This phrase, *In this world, it's kill or be killed,* will return again and again, more in theme than in literal text or dialogue. Since I'm

Undertale © Toby Fox

going to refer to it often as well, let's call it Flowey's Philosophy for consistency's sake. I think it'll help keep things running smooth.

Flowey is a personification of the literary term *juxtaposition*, which is when two story elements, characters, or concepts are placed next to each other to highlight their differences.

As a yellow flower, Flowey is a symbol of innocence, love, and beauty. Even the name Flowey is a further infantilization to contradict what he represents in the story. He opposes what he symbolizes, an innocent flower, by being a villain. The purpose of contrasting Flowey's character with his image is to make him stand out. If Flowey first appeared to Frisk as a slimy ogre that wanted to kill them, or an evil wizard, then his introduction wouldn't be nearly as memorable.

The LV, or LOVE, Flowey talks about actually stands for level of violence, and according to him, the higher your LOVE, the more EXP, or extermination points, you get. This is different from other

RPGs, where the player collects EXP, or experience points, from killing enemies, to raise their LV, or their level. Flowey represents this tradition in RPGs, where the player kills things to grow stronger, hence his Philosophy, "in this world, it's kill or be killed."

This also means Flowey's Philosophy is directly juxtaposed to the true pacifist route, which, to remind you, is the promise that you can beat the game without killing anything. Flowey's character takes on new meaning when he reveals his true nature as the antagonist and tells Frisk that his promise is a lie.

This opening is a great example of establishing expectations, then quickly subverting them. In one succinct encounter, Flowey sets a striking tone for the rest of the game and presents the challenging obstacle: that you *can't* beat *Undertale* without killing anything. Flowey's Philosophy proves that he is an unreliable narrator. Usually when someone tells you a story, you can trust that what they tell you is the truth (at least in the world of the story), but when you have an unreliable narrator, that isn't the case. Sometimes the narrator is wrong or mistaken or confused or, as in Flowey's case, just outright lying.

And Flowey's example, so early on in the game, warns the player to think twice about the things they see and hear in the Underground. As the protagonist, Frisk's main goal is to return home. It is up to the player to decide whether it's important to them to accept Flowey's Philosophy. And the game quickly shows them how with the introduction of a new character.

The moment before Flowey's second wave of projectiles hit Frisk, a cow-like monster with a gentle demeanor comes to their rescue by flicking the irritable plant away. Comfortingly, she takes

Frisk's hand and introduces herself as Toriel. She guides Frisk through the ruins and warns them of dangerous monsters like Flowey. Toriel suggests that if Frisk ever enters combat again, they should "strike up a friendly conversation" and wait for Toriel to resolve the conflict.

This humorous method of introducing how combat works subverts the expectation that you should defend yourself by fighting and instead offers the chance to become best buddies with your enemies. And if they're aggressive like Flowey and won't stop trying to kill you, then you should wait for Toriel to show up and handle things. It also subverts the expectation that there should be any type of combat at all in a game that promises you can complete it without killing a single enemy.

Undertale © Toby Fox

At first, Toriel seems like the archetypal mother/caretaker character. These characters typically serve a very limited role. In many RPGs, the mother, teary-eyed, waves the player off as they begin their great adventure. Occasionally, this type of character dies tragically to spur the hero on in their quest. In *Zelda Wind Waker*, it's his grandmother; in *Pokémon*, there is always a mother waiting for you at home as you explore the world. But *Undertale* subverts expectations yet again with Toriel, who literally holds Frisk's hand through the first few dangerous puzzles, but then on three separate occasions tells Frisk to wait until she returns, before abandoning them in their time of need. But no matter how long the player waits for Toriel, she never comes back. The only way for the game to continue is for Frisk to disobey her orders and make their own way.

Eventually, Frisk wanders through the ruins long enough to find a concerned Toriel waiting at her modest, suburban-looking house. Toriel is a little upset that Frisk didn't listen to her instructions but proud that they made it to her house on their own. She takes care of the child, gives them a room, and bakes them a pie. How much more motherly could you get?

The next morning, when Frisk asks when they can return home, Toriel tells them it's not possible. When Frisk asks why, Toriel says it's because the Underground is too dangerous for a child, so they must stay in her house forever to be safe.

Once again, the game definitively encourages the player to explore on their own, to look for answers outside of Toriel, and expect the unexpected. Unlike typical RPG mother figures, who are sad but understanding when their young children decide to leave home, Toriel is not willing to let Frisk go without a fight.

Toriel's determination to keep Frisk safe is so extreme that she is willing to physically force them to stay. Frisk demands Toriel let them go, but she refuses. Instead, she tells Frisk that they'll have to kill her to leave. You may be thinking that this is a little too extreme. But trust me, it's all for a purpose. There is no way these design decisions are an accident. Toby Fox knows exactly how far he needs to exaggerate Flowey's and Toriel's character features, not only to make them instantly memorable but also to provide proper commentary on role-playing video game tropes.

Toriel engages the player in battle, and the dialogue box appears with two options, to slay or spare. This is the first major choice the player is given in the game. If you choose to spare Toriel, the game forces you to stay by attacking you. And the battle never stops. Try as you might, you cannot evade Toriel's attacks forever, and eventually your health is chipped down to just two hit points, reminiscent of your first encounter with Flowey. The difference here, though, is that Toriel is not willing to land the final blow. Even if the player tries to hit her "friendliness pellets," they will dance around Frisk's heart, making it impossible to take any lethal damage. Toriel relents after you choose spare nearly twenty times. She never intended to kill Frisk; this whole conflict was about keeping the child safe. And perhaps realizing the irony of her actions, of harming Frisk in order to protect them, as well as seeing their determination to leave, causes her to stop fighting.

Toriel becomes emotionally exhausted when she realizes what she has done to Frisk. As a way of an apology, and also because she knows Frisk would be unhappy if they stayed in the ruins forever, she decides to let them go, but not without a warning. We find out that Toriel has seen six other humans come through the ruins to try to escape the Underground, and all of them have died at the hands of her ex-husband, Asgore, king of the Underground, a true monster. Toriel did everything in her power to save them, but time and again she has failed.

"Pathetic, is it not? I cannot save even a single child," she pines. Understanding her motivation, but unwilling to stay forever, Frisk leaves Toriel's home. Bitter, she makes them promise never to see or speak to her again.

Immediately after Frisk leaves the ruins, Flowey reappears. He repeats his Philosophy. Even though they made it past Toriel without killing or being killed, Frisk cannot escape the Underground without Flowey's Philosophy. There is a reason no human who has tried to escape the Underground has survived. According to Flowey, none of them were strong enough to kill. But I felt spurred on by the peaceful resolution of my encounter with Toriel and wanted to believe I could escape without having to sacrifice my morality.

Alternatively, to bypass Toriel, the player could have slayed her, giving in to Flowey's Philosophy, and any future interactions you would have had with this beloved mother-like character disappear. It's honestly surprising for some players that it's even possible to kill Toriel in the first place. After all, you were powerless in Flowey's grasp, and she was powerful enough to banish him with the flick of a wrist. The player's entire experience with Toriel is delicately covered in Bubble Wrap, designed to keep you from experiencing difficulty of any kind until your fight with her. The fact that you can be responsible for this protector's death develops the tone of this lighthearted game into having tangible, heartbreaking consequences.

Sparing Toriel or any of the other monsters you meet in the game is harder. Not only does Frisk have to spend more time surviving their attacks, but they also don't gain LV or EXP to help them in future battles. But although Frisk stays at the same power level, the player gains more intangible rewards. The game will often share the monster's motivations and tell you more about their lives after you spare them. You come to understand who the monsters are and what they want, and you can sympathize with them, interact with them again in the future, and feel good when you help them.

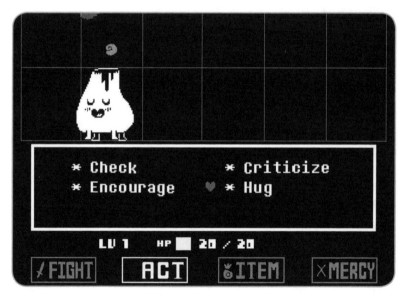

Undertale © Toby Fox

The encounter with Toriel is a template for two major choices throughout the game: to slay or to spare. Killing Toriel is easier, and after attempting to do so and failing, the game will spare her and allow Frisk to leave her house and adventure into the Underground. On my travels, I was charmed instantly by characters like Papyrus and Sans, skeleton brothers who are both named after the fonts their dialogue appears in. Sans especially captured my heart with a "pull my finger" joke. I was pursued relentlessly by Undyne, an intense fishlike monster who endearingly calls Frisk "*a wimpy loser with a big heart.*" And Alphys, the royal scientist, guided me through the hotlands in her own special way by introducing me to her literal human-killing machine, Mettaton the robot. Fox paid a special degree of attention to give every character their own story line, including making it possible to date Papyrus, Undyne, and Alphys. Funnily enough, to get the true pacifist ending, Frisk needs to date all three of them. There's no way I can do the individual and complex characters I've just mentioned justice in this book, but they each have their own personalities, desires, fears, fighting styles, and unique soundtracks. Depending on which type of route you choose, exploring all of them, neutral, pacifist, and genocide, will give you a more complete picture of everyone.

Undertale © Toby Fox

If you ever have the misfortune to get on Sans's bad side, he unexpectedly unleashes an unforgiving barrage of attacks, which kicks off perhaps one of the most meme-famous video game tracks of all time, "Megalomaniac." Papyrus, who wants nothing more than to capture a human to be promoted in the royal guard, uses his "fabled blue attack," which starts the song "Bonetrousle." You dodge and block arrows thrown by Undyne to "Spear of Justice."

Meeting and adventuring with this colorful cast of characters changed my goal, from becoming the strongest person in the Underground in order to return home to learning how to fit in with this community and to do right by these lovable monsters. Most of the fulfilling parts of *Undertale* are discovered while you make new friends during the true pacifist route.

As I mentioned before, there are multiple endings for *Undertale*, which adds to its complex nature and begs for multiple play-throughs. Each has its unique impact and message, but if I were to go through all of them here, this chapter would be . . . well, it'd be a bit much. But I want to touch on some aspects of the neutral and genocide endings, because *Undertale* uses some fascinating storytelling techniques that are really powerful in video games. For example, breaking the fourth wall.

After completing a neutral route, Flowey, for example, taunts, encourages, or pleads with the player to return to the game to get a more satisfactory ending through the true pacifist route. And Sans, who becomes one of your closest friends during the pacifist route, condemns you if you choose the genocide route and becomes the true final boss. Before he dies, he directs his final words to you, the player: "No matter what, you'll just keep going. Not out of any desire for good or evil . . . but just because you think you can. And because you *can*, you *have to*." His eerie farewell made me feel as if he were reading my mind, because I *was* just completing tasks to get the genocide ending. It made me reconsider what I was doing and gave all my future decisions more weight.

Undertale also does some impressive things that are only possible in video games, like applying long-lasting effects to the consequences of your decisions, even after completing the game multiple times, to give them meaning. Other games that try to make your choices matter, like *BioShock* and *Red Dead Redemption II*, use a fluid morality system and gauge goodness versus badness on a scale. Don't want to be a bad guy anymore? Simply donate to charity! Don't want to be a good guy anymore? Have some fun and give in to your worst instincts! *Undertale* sets itself apart by making your choices affect characters you genuinely care about in such permanent ways they're nearly impossible to reverse without resetting your save file, but even then, astoundingly, the game remembers what you've done in the past.

For example, the genocide route is by far the quickest to complete because you team up with Flowey and he helps you skip obstacles. The challenging part for me became forcing myself to do some terribly evil things just to get the ending I wanted, like annihilating some of my favorite characters and watching their tiny hearts snap in two or melt away while they begged for mercy. The music becomes distorted, and characters like Sans and Toriel comment on how they need to protect the world from you. After completing a genocide run, Flowey tells the player their save file is so corrupted that the only way to reset it is by selling their soul. If you do reset your game, characters will mention how they remember the horrible things you did in your past life. And if you do everything correctly the second time to try to get a true pacifist ending, you won't be able to because you didn't have a soul to begin with.

Undertale is designed to make you feel as if it knows what you're thinking by watching every step you take. Major decisions you make have ripple effects of consequences with such consistent internal logic the world comes to life. The game holds you accountable in meaningful ways by affecting characters in the Underground that you care about.

Even though the alternatively dark routes feel unsettling, it's amazing to experience how much life just one person can put into a video game when great storytelling design comes first. There is a lot to appreciate and learn from these twisted endings, but the most fulfilling experiences I had with the game were when I spared everyone I met in the true pacifist route. And for that reason, I'll use this perspective to explain the rest of the story.

As I was seeking creative ways to spare my enemies, following the true pacifist route, I learned many of the game's hidden secrets, lore, and the real story of how the monsters ended up in the Underground. And the more I learned, the stronger Flowey's Philosophy felt. If I wanted to leave, I would have to slay eventually.

The story centers on the royal family and King Asgore Dreemurr's quest to avenge his son, Asriel, who was tragically murdered by humans after his escape from the Underground. As I was fighting Asgore, the character I believed was the final boss, I spared him in pursuit of the true pacifist ending. But the result wasn't exactly happy. It was . . . lukewarm. Asgore eventually saw the errors in his logic and became willing to end his quest to avenge his son, and by choosing to spare Asgore, Frisk could live in the Underground forever. I believed I had done the right thing, even though it would mean Frisk never returns home and the monsters would remain trapped with no hope of freedom.

Up until this point, I had constantly denied taking the fastest path to the finish line in order to get the true pacifist ending. The takeaway is obvious: Doing what's right isn't always easy, and sometimes that means sacrificing getting what you want. Even if what you want might not be inherently wrong; even if you might just want to go home. I thought this lukewarm ending was telling me that if getting what I wanted meant sacrificing my morals, then it wasn't worth it. If returning home meant I had to kill Asgore, I wasn't going to do it, even though he'd done horrible things. And if the game was ending here, then I could live with that.

That was when Flowey appeared and killed the wounded king. And then my game crashed.

Toby Fox used every tool at his disposal to surprise the player when building Undertale's brain, including shutting the story down after a dramatic scene. This moment highlights one of the most important aspects of storytelling in video games that makes this genre unique, that the medium the player interacts with has a mind of its own.

At first, when my game crashed, I thought it was some kind of bug, but the timing was too coincidental for that. I rebooted Undertale and was shocked to discover that Flowey had transformed into a demented demon more powerful than Asgore himself, known as Photoshop Flowey. This is another example of how Toby Fox establishes expectations, progresses toward them, and right at the last moment, pulls the rug out from under the audience.

Undertale © Toby Fox

But it's one thing for a storyteller to pull off an unexpected twist. It's another to resolve that newfound conflict satisfactorily. Fox made sure to signpost from the very beginning of *Undertale*'s story that it's possible to spare every character in the game and that "in this world, it's kill or be killed" comes from the mouth of Flowey himself. Then he escalates the tension in a crescendo from beginning to end and concludes the melody gracefully to make the player feel as if they've finally arrived home.

Sparing Photoshop Flowey was one of the most rewarding, heartfelt experiences I've had in gaming. If you choose to spare Flowey, then you get one step closer to the true pacifist ending and experience one of the biggest twists in the game (if not the biggest twist), that Flowey is actually a heartless reincarnation of Asriel Dreemurr, the king's long-lost son. Asriel absorbs all the souls in the Underground, including those of all your friends, to break the barrier and travel to the surface to take over the world. He just needs one more human soul to accomplish his goal. Asriel tries to kill Frisk, but if you evade his attacks long enough, you can spare him as well. I'll leave the details of that juicy conclusion for you to discover on your own, however. It's worth it, and if you're a fan of story games, which I'm guessing by the book in your hands that you are, then experiencing this ending yourself is a gift you deserve.

Undertale is about morality. And I can't think of any medium better than video games to explore that topic, because of the interactivity. The player must participate and become complicit in the game's results.

In the beginning, the game poses a question: In the Underground, is it "kill or be killed"? This phrase is reminiscent of another: It's a dog-eat-dog world. It encourages a certain way of life, a drive to get what you want, no matter the cost. Because if you don't get yours first, then the worst thing could happen and someone else could get *your* dream. Achieve the goals *you* wanted to achieve. This philosophy made Flowey strong. Think about how Frisk grows when you raise their LV and EXP, and what those things stand for. And according to Flowey, not only is this the right thing to do, it's the only thing that can bring happiness.

Undertale's answer to that question is that when you harm others, you're only harming yourself. The more powerful Flowey grew, the more heartless he became. The same is true for Frisk when you go the genocide route. Even though it was easier, and my stats grew rapidly, the Underground grew colder. It didn't lead to more happiness, it didn't even lead to more pain, it just led to a lack of feeling. To nothingness. To emptiness. When you serve yourself, you may find that you've become more powerful (more money, more things, greater status), but that you've distanced yourself from the things that make you human, your emotions.

Undertale © Toby Fox

At the risk of sounding cliché, *Undertale* taught me that life is worth living, not because of the things you can get, but because of the things you can give. Unlike the other routes, the true pacifist ends with all the monsters spared, including Flowey/Asriel, finally free of their prison and watching the sunrise. Even Toriel is there and willing to speak to you again, and she and Frisk start a new life together on the surface. That happy ending wouldn't have been possible if I'd just taken everything I wanted. Even though the journey wasn't as easy, it was far, far more enjoyable.

I can understand why people who've played *Undertale* and only got a neutral ending would be confused as to why it's such a big deal. Sure, the music is incredible, and there's great dog and snail humor. If this was all *Undertale* had to offer, it'd be a very good, above average RPG, right? But luckily for us, it's anything but average. *Undertale*, played to completion, every digital page of this book fully discovered, will reveal one thing.

Undertale is a masterpiece.

BOOK REPORT:

Final Fantasy VII

Final Fantasy VII © Square Enix

INITIAL RELEASE DATE AND PLATFORM:

January 1997 for the PlayStation

WHERE ELSE CAN IT BE FOUND?

Luckily, if you want to play this game, it can be found just about everywhere. PSP, PS4, Android, Xbox One, Nintendo Switch, and iOS all have versions you can check out. In 2020, the *FFVII Remake* edition became the first release of a planned series to bring this game to a whole new audience on the PlayStation 4 and PlayStation 5.

Category:

Linear Narrative, Action Role-Playing Game

Main Characters:

Cloud Strife, the game's protagonist. A troubled mercenary who joins with an eco-terrorist group to stop Shinra from draining the life of the Planet to use as an energy source.

Tifa Lockhart, childhood friend of Cloud and heroine of *Final Fantasy VII*. She is one of the lead members of AVALANCHE and initially persuades Cloud to join them in their rebellion against Shinra.

Aerith Gainsborough, a member of AVALANCHE and the last surviving Cetra, or "Ancient," one of the planet's oldest races

Sephiroth, the main antagonist. Originally he was a member of Shinra's SOLDIER elite, but a traumatic incident involving his true origins drove him insane.

Setting:

The planet of Gaia, referred to simply as "the Planet" by its inhabitants, has three main continents. The planet is a living organism, and its lifeblood is the Lifestream, the liquid form being Mako, which wells in the substrata. Above the surface, Mako crystallizes into Materia, which allows its users to manipulate the powers of the planet in a phenomenon many call magic. But harvesting Mako as an energy source drains the planet of its life and corrupts life-forms, creating monsters in the wild.

Story Summary:

Shinra, a corrupt organization, has the entire world tricked into believing it is the only source of good. Except for AVALANCHE, a group of ordinary people who banded together to fight back against the powerful corporation. They come into their own when

Tifa Lockhart persuades her childhood friend Cloud Strife, a talented but disgraced ex-SOLDIER in search of revenge, to join the cause. Over the course of many missions and adventures, the group is joined by an expanding cast of characters, including Aerith, a flower seller with the ability to speak to the earth.

But their mission changes when Sephiroth, a menacing figure from Cloud's past, slaughters the president of Shinra Inc. and reveals the much more dangerous truth that the corporation was hiding. Now Cloud and his friends must hunt Sephiroth down and destroy him before he can summon the end of the world.

WHY THE REMAKE? WHAT'S DIFFERENT?

Final Fantasy VII Remake © *Square Enix*

Quite a bit, actually. The most obvious change is the graphics. This isn't a simple case of slapping on a few new textures and calling it good. No, *Final Fantasy VII Remake* is stunning. All new art from top to bottom that really shows off the power of new hardware, while expanding on the original story. Much as the Lord of the Rings movies stretched *The Hobbit* into three feature-length movies, *FFVII Remake* splits up the original game into multiple games. In fact, *Remake* focuses on some events that happened *before* the original even started, so there's quite a bit to dig into here. If you want the whole story in a single sitting, you'll have to play the original version, but if you're patient and have a few years, the graphics improvement and the details you'll find pre-Midgar (if you know, you know) in the remake might be worth the wait.

WHAT DID YOU THINK OF THIS STORY?

Okay, admission time. This one hits my nostalgia more than just about any game in this book. It was the first 3D Final Fantasy game, which kind of blew my mind at the time. Although, if I'm being really honest here, it isn't even my favorite FF game (I like 4 and 6 better from a gameplay side of things). But this story was just . . . so tuned and perfect. The atmosphere, the music, there were both new and familiar characters from previous games, and the conflict was so perfectly balanced. Cloud Strife is a conflicted character, but we fall for him because he is pitted against what many gamers still call one of the greatest villains in video game history, Sephiroth.

So, nostalgia matters when it comes to favorites, but in the end this is a fantastic story with unforgettable characters, an all-time great soundtrack, set in a stunning and memorable world. What's not to love?

POV

To put it in the most simple terms, point of view, or POV, refers to who is telling the story. Like most things in art, there is some disagreement as to how many types of point of view there are, but it's generally accepted that there are three, with a bit of a twist on the third.

FIRST-PERSON POV IS WHEN ONE OF THE CHARACTERS in the story acts as the narrator. This is generally revealed by the "I" sentence construction and relies on first-person pronouns. ("I went to the bank.")

Second-person POV is structured around the "you" pronoun. Some refer to this as the "instructional POV," and it is much less common than first and third ("You thought it was time to go to the bank.")

In third-person POV, the author narrates a story about the characters and refers to them with third-person pronouns, "he/she/they." (She arrived at noon, then robbed the bank.)

This POV, however, is subdivided. It can be third-person omniscient or third-person limited. While both adhere to the third-person pronoun rule, there are some important differences. In third-person limited (often called "close third"), the author sticks closely to one character, giving readers the ability to read the thoughts of this single character in a story. In contrast, third-person omniscient is broader, allowing the narrator to know everything about the story and its characters, often hopping freely from the mind of one character to another.

I've added this section, which might feel like a refresher course to many, for another reason. I really want to quickly point out that these POVs play a really interesting role in media in general, and in games specifically.

It's fair to say that film and TV are the most limited in their approach to POV. While there are instances of first and second POV in this medium, they are extremely rare. The bulk of what you see in film falls into the third-person POV category.

Comics are similar. They are often delivered in third-person POV. I can think of a few, and I mean few, examples of first-person POV comics, but they were really experimental pieces. And honestly, they didn't really make a splash in the market. It's just—well— visually not that great to look through the eyes of the character in a film, TV show, or comic. I think a big part of this is that we are used to the first-person POV in real life. We have full control to look around, close our eyes, or focus in on details that are personally meaningful to us in the moment. In film and comics, this is simply not possible.

Books are actually really great at all three major POVs. They get past the restricted, limited first-person POV problem that comics and film present because all the imagery happens in the reader's imagination. Books are great at asking us to step into the character's head in first person, because we often refer to ourselves in first person in our inner thoughts. Second person, while still rare and very challenging to write, can allow you to draw your reader into the story and make them feel as if they are part of the action because the narrator is speaking directly to them. And third person, both omniscient and limited, is super common in books because we want to experience what it's like to live someone's life that is different from ours.

But games, well, that's where we start to see some really cool and experimental stuff happening.

First-person POV in games fixes the limited-camera problem presented in film and comics as well. In first-person games, we see through the player's eyes. As we flick the mouse around, the camera moves, becoming a surrogate for the player's head, allowing us full control of the viewable world presented to us. And when we pump high-quality, directional audio in through headphones or a sound system, we can become even more immersed in the experience.

Seeing other characters in the world look directly at you and address you in first person in a game really makes you *feel* like the protagonist. It's a singularly unique experience in media, and when it's done right, it can be outstanding.

Games like *Half-Life, BioShock, Overwatch,* and *Call of Duty* all fall into the first-person shooter category, as gunplay takes precedence over the bulk of the action. But shooters aren't the only genre that benefits from first-person perspective.

Portal and *Portal 2, The Witness, Firewatch,* and *Gone Home* are some of the most immersive and interesting story games out there, and they take full advantage of this POV. And when I played the indie game *The Beginner's Guide,* I not only played the game as a first-person character, I was literally a character in the game. It's a bizarre experience to say the least to feel as if the game has been created just for you, and once again, something that is fully unique to the gaming world.

Second-person POV games are more rare now, but they have a long history in the game world. For years, before graphics dominated gaming, text adventures were often presented as second-person POV experiences. Games like *Colossal Cave Adventure*, *The Hitchhiker's Guide to the Galaxy*, and *Planetfall* nailed this presentation. And who can forget *Zork*, with its haunting line of "You are likely to be eaten by a grue."

And while it isn't a video game, it's worth mentioning that Dungeons and Dragons is played in second-person POV. The dungeon master provides instructions in second person constantly . . . "You found a treasure. You woke up an orc. You are now orc food."

The Stanley Parable, a game created by Davey Wreden, the genius behind *The Beginner's Guide* mentioned above, takes a very literal approach to a second-person narrative. *The Stanley Parable*'s narrator comments on things you do in the game. If you push the number six on a number pad, the narrator will say, "Stanley pushed the number six." And when you do something questionable in the game, it isn't out of place to hear the narrator comment, "Why would you do that?" It's a unique approach and was effective enough for *The Stanley Parable* to do very well, both in the market and in the awards circuit.

And if you really want an excellent example of this POV in games, then *Trover Saves the Universe* is worth a gander. I played it in VR, and while the language was full-on adult (you've been warned), this game was intentionally awkward, nearly impossible to control, and flat-out one of the most hilarious games I've ever played. Leave it to Justin Roiland and Squanch Games to push boundaries and make something so wacky that it fits perfectly in line with the rest of Justin's portfolio. In addition to being the head cheese at Squanch, Justin is also a cocreator of *Rick and Morty* and a voice actor and cocreator on Hulu's *Solar Opposites*. He's a fantastic storyteller, and watching him take his talents back and forth from television to games has been a blast.

Trover Saves the Universe © Squanch Games

And I'm sure you're already thinking ahead of me here, but third-person POV is really common in games. It's such a widely used POV that games even break it down to playstyle categories. Isometric (*Hades, Divinity: Original Sin, Diablo* . . .), platformers (*Celeste, Hollow Knight, Super Mario Bros.* . . . .), over-the-shoulder shooters (*The Last of Us, Uncharted, Red Dead Redemption, Zelda* . . .), and so on. Basically, any game where you're able to see your character or vehicle on screen from above, behind, or from the side can be considered third-person POV.

The POV used in games not only dramatically changes how the story is delivered, but it also alters how the game itself is played. *Call of Duty: Modern Warfare* would work as an isometric shooter, but it would be totally wrong for the up close, personal experience the game is trying to deliver. And while you could make a first-person version of Mario, it just wouldn't seem right to slip inside Mario's head, to hear his internal thoughts as he deals with Champion's Road in *Super Mario 3D*. Not to mention how difficult the controls would be if you weren't able to see the world's most famous plumber moving around the world from behind. I mean . . . that would be just wrong, right?

BOOK REPORT:

The Witcher 3: Wild Hunt

The Witcher 3: Wild Hunt © CD Project Red

INITIAL RELEASE DATE AND PLATFORM:

May 2015 for PC, PlayStation 4, Xbox One

WHERE ELSE CAN IT BE FOUND?

The Witcher 3 was released on Nintendo Switch in October 2019.

Fun Fact:

The Witcher 3 takes advantage of video game interactivity and allows the player's choices to affect the narrative. Interestingly, it's actually based on the Witcher Saga, a book series by Polish author Andrzej Sapkowski.

Category:

Nonlinear Narrative, Action Role-Playing Game

Main Characters:

Geralt of Rivia, Witcher, monster slayer for hire, and protagonist

Yennefer of Vengerberg, sorceress and Geralt's love interest

Cirilla of Cintra, Geralt's ward and the Lady of the Worlds

Setting:

The game is set on the Continent, a massive open world that traverses multiple kingdoms built with incredible attention to detail. The story takes place during a war between the empire of Nilfgaard and the Northern Kingdoms, and the player can explore major cities like Novigrad, the no man's land of Velen, and the Redanian city of Oxenfurt. The camera is in third person, and Geralt takes up a small part of the middle of the screen. That way, he is always the center of attention and we are allowed to see the vast world in front of us.

Story Summary:

Geralt of Rivia, the world's best tracker, is enlisted by Emperor Emhyr to find his daughter, the princess Cirilla Fiona Elen Riannon. To most people, however, she is known as Ciri. To Geralt, she was his ward, trained to be a Witcher, who became somewhat of a daughter to him. The story picks up nearly two decades after her apprenticeship, as she is being chased by the Wild Hunt, an otherworldly elvish army hungrily seeking the ancestral power that resides in Ciri. A child of the Elderblood, Cirilla is the last in an Elven bloodline that gives its descendants power to travel through space and time. If the Wild Hunt had that power, they could mobilize their armies through dimensions and conquer the universes. It's up to Geralt to find her first.

What Did You Think of This Story?

What sets *The Witcher 3* apart is being able to maintain a sense of awe at the scale of bringing such a huge open world to life. The attention to detail in this game is simply amazing. With a deep mainline story and hundreds of hours of side quests, this game feels massive. Yet it can still get down into fine details with things like *Gwent*, for example, a fully functioning deck-building card game that lives both inside and outside the game and is known to be the most popular game in the Continent.

But while making a fictional world come to life is an important part of storytelling, it has no power unless it's paired with characters who struggle with believable internal conflict. And there is no shortage of great characters here. There's Dandelion, Dijkstra, the Bloody Baron Phillip Strenger, Triss Merigold . . . But most importantly, the game has a compelling protagonist in Geralt, the star of the show.

Geralt isn't the chosen one in this story, his surrogate daughter, Ciri, is. And hours upon hours of the main story line are spent in pursuit of her, only finding traces here and there across the Continent. The game has missions, flashbacks of when young Ciri was being trained by Geralt, to help the player better understand their relationship. There are also missions when you play as Ciri, to understand her internal struggles as she is being chased through dimensions by the Wild Hunt. It's a moment of relief when Geralt and Ciri eventually do reunite, but their time together is precious, because the Wild Hunt is always close behind.

Once you start reading into the many world-building details of high-fantasy stories like *The Witcher 3*, it's not uncommon to feel a bit overwhelmed. Not because world-building and fantasy aren't fun—most of my favorite stories are set in these unbelievably magical places. But because emotion comes from meaning. While the Wild Hunt, the war splitting the Continent in half, and the details of Ciri's ancient powers are important to explain so the characters in the story make decisions that make sense, you need a sympathetic protagonist to make players care, and *The Witcher 3* does this beautifully by building deep relationships between Geralt and all the surrounding characters.

When you eventually reach that final battle with the Wild Hunt, the player can choose how Geralt helps Ciri prepare, and the decisions they make, up until the moment when Ciri must go alone to fight them, will determine the type of ending the player receives. There were so many times while I was playing *The Witcher 3* that I sat there, paused, for several minutes debating which choice I should make because I cared about these characters, and I didn't want to make a decision that ruined their relationship. And the final choice Geralt must make regarding Ciri's sacrifice was one I debated for a long time. It's one I hope you eventually struggle to make yourself.

Situational Irony (N.)

Irony involving a situation in which actions have an effect that is opposite from what was intended, so that the outcome is contrary to what was expected. A plot twist.

KNOW WE INCLUDED A SPOILER WARNING EARLIER for the entire book, but for this game in particular, I think it's important to say it again. ***There will be spoilers here.***

BioShock has one of the greatest plot-twist endings in video game history. (A bold claim, but I'll defend it anytime!) This is a game where the experience of discovery, of learning the truth, is key. And in discussing the ending, in revealing that plot twist, I'm taking away your chance to discover.

So, if you haven't played *BioShock* yet, you might want to stop reading now and come back later.

The other reason the game should be played is that it's just freaking awesome. It's rated M, with a lot of language and disturbing imagery, so make sure you're old enough and ready for that, but the gameplay is top-notch. It's a first-person shooter (a term we will discuss more later) and a gothic horror game with well-placed and terrifying jump scares that keep you on your digital toes, but it's so much more than that.

In 1960, an airplane is flying over the mid-Atlantic. Our player character, Jack, is sitting alone, looking nostalgically at an old photograph of his parents he keeps in his wallet. We hear his gravelly voice say, "They told me, son, you're special. You were born to do great things."

Jack holds up a wrapped present with a handwritten note that reads, *To Jack with love, from Mom & Dad. Would you kindly not open—*. The rest of the note is covered by a large red ribbon.

Jack continues his monologue, "You know what? They were right."

Then screaming fills the air as the plane begins to shake. The screen goes black, and the whine of the propellers grows until we hear the crash and roaring splash of the airplane meeting the ocean. The word *BIOSHOCK* appears, rising up from the black, and water trickles down the art deco–style logo.

And that is the only time we hear Jack's voice. We inhabit him for the next however many hours, but those four sentences are the only words we ever hear him speak.

It's worth pointing out here that this technique, the silent protagonist, is something that video games do particularly well. And *BioShock* isn't alone here by a long shot. RPGs do it so often it's almost a rule, and games like *Half-Life* and *Half-Life 2* and the *Portal* games also use this technique masterfully. It's designed to allow us to slide into the character in a more seamless manner. Removing the voice of the character, or their thoughts, helps us believe we are Jack, in the case of *BioShock*, and encourages his thoughts to become ours.

Another thing that allows us to slide into the role of Jack is that the game is played in first person, making it easier for us to identify with the main character. Not only do we never hear from Jack again verbally, but we never actually see what Jack looks like, either. All we see are his hands as they move in front of the camera, hold weapons, open doors, and the like.

This first-person point of view is particularly important in *BioShock* because it also gives us a greater feeling of agency as we play. We can walk anywhere and interact with objects how we'd like; we can even choose to avoid conflict. And we make these decisions in our minds, then control the character, Jack, to do whatever we choose. This sense of agency helps instill a sense of responsibility for the choices we make as we continue to uncover the story.

The logo fades away, and Jack sinks underwater. He swims through plane wreckage toward the surface. Jet fuel floats on top of the ocean, ablaze in orange plumes, offering enough flickering light for him to see a lighthouse rising in the middle of the ocean. Jack makes his way there, the lone survivor, and finds the door open. As he enters, music from the forties floats softly from below, and a looming statue of a grumpy-looking man stares down at him, covered by a red banner with gold lettering reading NO GODS OR KINGS. ONLY MAN.

BioShock © 2K Games

Soaking wet, Jack gingerly follows the music to the basement
of the lighthouse and discovers a small, round pod of brass and
glass. With nowhere else to go, he enters the pod to investigate.
The door closes behind him, and the vehicle plunges deep into the
ocean. Then a video screen turns on and plays an old 8mm-style
film. Black-and-white illustrations of happy people smoking glowing cigarettes as music and narration chime at you through a tiny
speaker. The image changes to a man named Andrew Ryan smoking
a pipe. "Is a man not entitled to the sweat of his brow?" He goes
on to admonish Washington, a representation of the American
government; the Vatican, a representation of religion and god; and
Moscow, a representation of communism. As Ryan's voice grows
more and more animated, he professes that he rejects all those
beliefs. What Andrew Ryan believes in is something different. "I
chose the impossible. I chose . . . Rapture. A city where the artist
would not be censored. Where the scientist would not be bound

by petty morality. Where the great would not be constrained by the small. And with the sweat of your brow, Rapture can become your city as well."

This opening sets the tone for the game to come as the television screen rolls up to reveal the underwater utopia Andrew Ryan created. Massive art deco buildings glow with elaborate neon signs as a whale gracefully navigates between them. The visual feast this game provides in its opening minutes as you go from a fiery crash to the lavish interior of the lighthouse to this vast view of an underground supercity filled with impossible-to-believe ocean life was stunning in 2007, and it still holds up today.

In writing, there's a popular phrase that often gets tossed around: *Show, don't tell.* In literature that means it's better to describe visually what is happening, to define a situation by its surroundings and outcomes, or to have your characters emote and react, rather than just spell things out. Generally, games are good at this, being that they are an inherently visual medium, but *BioShock* takes this to a whole different level, by letting us experience huge portions of the story with very little dialogue.

So much is said in this game through the tone and setting. The art deco–inspired architecture, the music that brings us back to days gone by, and the constant, claustrophobic feeling caused by leaking walls and pipes and the occasional large fish swimming by at eye level; none of them are discussed in proper dialogue, but all add to the story.

Which is not to say that there isn't a lot of great dialogue in *BioShock* that also plays an important role in setting the mood. Most of what you hear in the game is gathered through audio recordings, and the voices and language used fit right in with the time period. Within a few minutes, you start to pick up on the unique vernacular, almost like a slang, that gives you a sense of the oddities in the world of Rapture.

Two voices from an overhead loudspeaker discuss the crash at the lighthouse while Jack floats through the beautiful city. At first, I'll admit, I was comforted knowing I wasn't alone. The underwater world has always been a bit creepy to me, and up to this point, I was feeling a bit lonely. But that quickly ends when terror fills the disembodied voices as they talk about something called Splicers and mention they are approaching quickly. Jack's pod, which is called the bathysphere (don't you just love that name?), docks in a glass tube with white neon words reading, ALL GOOD THINGS OF THIS EARTH FLOW INTO THE CITY. But as the pod reaches an air lock, the awe and beauty of discovering an entirely new world is shattered as we meet our first Splicer. The Splicers are the most common survivors of Rapture's population, which isn't good for anyone. They are addicted to a gene-splicing wonder drug called ADAM, and they have been left hideously deformed and hopelessly insane as a result. Their appearance is still humanlike, but their humanity was drained long ago.

You watch helplessly as the Splicer backs a human inhabitant of the undersea world into a dark hallway. The lights, which are flickering at best, and black as pitch at their worst, show you just enough of what happens to the man as he begs for his life. The Splicer rips him in two, showering the hallway with blood, then the lights go out to save us from seeing what he does next. However, your ears don't lie as the gurgling and chomping continue. But things only get worse when the Splicer notices Jack in his glass bubble. It looks directly into the camera and says, in an eerie, barely human voice, "Is it someone new?", followed by a scream meant to give a thousand nightmares. Then it jumps on top of Jack's transport and begins tearing at the glass-and-metal hull. Let me just say, this moment was terrifying. There is something extra eerie about a modified superbaddie that speaks to you. Seriously, I still get shivers today as I think about this moment. Shivers!

Before the Splicer can enter the pod, the portal on the bathysphere opens and Jack hears a voice coming from a radio. He enters Rapture to grab the radio and is introduced to a man named Atlas, the next major character in the game. Atlas tells you his story, how he arrived in Rapture with his family, seeking the unbridled creativity and hope Ryan's city promised. But their once bright civilization toppled under Ryan's manic leadership. Atlas tells Jack that he's determined to keep him alive and that he needs him to help him and his family escape by submarine. Without a better option, you find it best to go with this stranger. After only a few minutes of chaos, finding direction, any direction, seems like not just the only but also the best option. Atlas tells Jack to get to higher ground and locate a submarine called *Neptune's Bounty.*

At first, the player doesn't really know what's going on here. All they know is that Ryan had a vision to create the perfect city, away from the constraints of government intervention. The citizens were obviously thriving at one point, but something went horribly wrong. The first few hours are a juxtaposition of beautiful architecture, holographic memories of better days gone by, and the horrific decay of something that can only be described as nightmarish human experimentation.

Objects and corpses are strewn about, and maniacal people roam the halls with little or no purpose other than to destroy everything they encounter. Atlas guides Jack through the chaos, battling through the enemy encounters with nothing more than a wrench, until he happens upon a vial of red something-or-other and a massive syringe. Without pause, Jack stabs himself with the syringe and pumps his bloodstream full of the red goo.

Let's stop here for just a second. This is a fantasy game. You are in an underwater city filled with murderous bad guys, for one thing. But even in a fantasy world like this, I found it odd at first that Jack would just blindly shoot up with some unknown substance. Why would he do that? Or more important, why would the game do that *for* me? Sure, we're playing a game, but it did feel a bit much, even in this strange setting, to just blindly trust this stuff. It was a bit off-putting for me the first time I played to not be able to choose whether I wanted to inject this stuff into my arm, but then I (and Jack) learned that this red stuff is called a plasmid and that it alters your genetic makeup to give you superpowers. This dose, for example, gives Jack the ability to shoot lightning out from his fingertips. There are a variety of plasmids as you make your way through the game, but they need to be powered up by another substance called EVE. If you think of the plasmid as a weapon, then EVE is the ammo.

But as amazing as these powers are, they come from a dark source. The plasmids are built from a genetic material called ADAM,

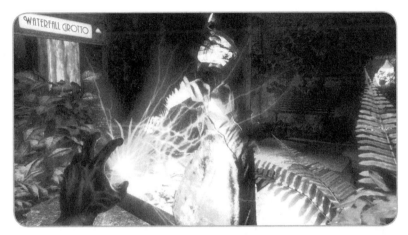

BioShock © 2K Games

which is collected from a rare sea slug found near Rapture. Upon discovery, the powers that the plasmids provided became all the rage in Rapture, and soon the demand for ADAM outpaced what could be collected from the slugs.

As Atlas says, "everybody wants ADAM, everybody needs it." Soon demand led to more scientific breakthroughs as it was discovered that the ADAM output from the slugs could be increased by twenty times if the slugs were implanted into a living human host.

But to make things worse, the only viable hosts for the sea slugs were young girls. Soon an orphanage offered up the poor girls for the good of Rapture, and they became known as Little Sisters. And to make the Little Sisters even more valuable, the production of ADAM inside their bellies also created a byproduct called EVE that could be used to power the plasmids. It was a vicious cycle that robbed the girls of their childhood in the most tragic of ways.

The Little Sisters are small and nearly defenseless, but if you or anyone else tries to attack them, they scream, summoning a hulking, half-machine, half-beast monstrosity to their aid. These are the other iconic enemy of *BioShock*, the Big Daddies, and their job is to keep the Little Sisters safe.

BioShock © 2K Games

Even with his new Thor-like powers, Jack grows more desperate following Atlas's advice. Finally, he's led to *Neptune's Bounty*, his one way out of the city. But before he can board and end this horrible nightmare, gates drop down from the ceiling and shut him off from the submarine and a screeching alarm attracts the Splicers. A mounted TV blinks to life and shows Andrew Ryan. He accuses Jack, the intruder, of being a CIA or KGB agent and wishes him a slow and painful death. His hopes of escape dashed, Jack panics while the Splicers' long shadows draw nearer. Fortunately, Atlas, who apparently has some modicum of control over the city's functions, unlocks a tiny escape hatch for Jack to descend deeper into Rapture. Jack might not be able to leave, but he will at least survive a little while longer.

Not long afterward, Jack runs into a major, moral decision. He meets Brigid Tenenbaum, a brilliant scientist who is the architect of ADAM, along with a few of her Little Sisters. Atlas, the constant voice in Jack's ear, tells him to kill one of the Little Sisters, saying, "They are barely human anymore. They are nothing more than genetically scrambled monsters, and killing them would be showing them some mercy." But Tenenbaum tells Jack she has been working to free the Little Sisters and has come up with a plasmid that will reverse the horrible things she and Yi Suchong, a doctor involved in their creation, have done to them. Jack backs one of the helpless little children into a corner, and Tenenbaum tosses you a vial that will set her free. The game gives the player two choices, "harvest or rescue" the Little Sister. One will help ease your conscience; one will make you more powerful in the game. This moment allows the player to determine Jack's destiny.

After making his choice, Jack continues his adventure. Eventually, Jack makes his way back to *Neptune's Bounty*, where he finds Atlas's family waiting for him on the submarine. It seems as if his journey through hell is coming to an end, until he hears a recognizable voice. Ryan greets him directly over the radio, then destroys the submarine and the innocent family on board. Jack survives the explosion and agrees when Atlas asks him, "would you kindly" help seek revenge on Ryan.

Everything we've discussed up to this point has all been in Jack's present, but to really understand the meat of this story, you have to know the backstory, the history of Rapture. As you play the game, it becomes clear that the overarching sociological aspects of Rapture and the history of this odd city play directly into Jack's story. But if it were told all at once, it would be too much, so the developers leak it to you a bit at a time through the use of audio diaries found throughout the fallen metropolis. It seems these personal audio-capture devices were all the rage, because Jack finds them scattered everywhere. And as he listens to them, he pieces together a narrative.

This patient drip of critical information the writers of *BioShock* use is really worth mentioning here because it's a fantastic writing tool. All too often, writers have a tendency to want to infodump all the context and world-building and backstory at once. To front-load it. And I get it, from a writing perspective. You want to make sure your reader, or gamer, or moviegoer knows all the juicy details you've dreamed up so they understand your every decision as fast as possible. But in reality, slamming all this info in front of us bogs down the action (or stops it completely), and instead of making the player care more about the story, it often has the unintended effect of making them less invested as they get bored with the influx of information and eager to get back to the characters and adventure they signed up for.

Through the audiotapes, we learn that Andrew Ryan was born just before the Russian Revolution in 1917. His childhood convinced him of one major thing, great men became great by their own efforts, not by relying on the government or anything else to rise to their station. He believed anything else made you a parasite. He moved to America at the age of nine, and his approach to life worked for him. He became very wealthy in the capitalist society that surrounded him, but over time the American government began to ask more and more of the wealthy to take care of those less fortunate. Ryan saw this as a failure, a reminder of his long-held concept of parasites feeding off his success, and he soured on the American vision.

This fundamental belief system that Andrew Ryan developed is similar to, if not a direct copy of Ayn Rand's philosophy of objectivism. The hints the developers put down were not subtle. Andrew Ryan is basically an anagram for Ayn Rand (We Ayn Rand), and the other character that plays a major part in this game, Atlas, shares the name of one of her most important works, *Atlas Shrugged*. I'm not going to go in depth into the philosophy of Rand and how it applies to *BioShock*, because that could be a book on its own, but I will say that basically it comes down to this: The only truth is that which we can see and understand, and that truth is absolute. What we can observe and prove exists, and what we cannot does not. This also elevates one's own self-interest to the highest order, because those who create a better existence for themselves deserve the fruits of their labors. The full philosophy is much more complicated than that, but this definition will get us through for now.

Whether the game supports or opposes the philosophy is up for debate, but the entire civilization of Rapture is based solely on objectivist concepts. Phew. That was a lot.

When the American government tried to claim a large portion of land Ryan owned to turn it into a national park, he burned it to the ground. But the thing that really broke Andrew Ryan was the atomic bomb in Hiroshima. He rationalized that now, with this power, the parasites, as he called them, could take anything they desired. In his view, this world was forfeit. So he used his fortune to build a new one. He gathered thousands of the best and brightest and offered them an opportunity to build the city of their dreams, without government overreach or restriction. No legal or moral restrictions, where their work could achieve greater limits than the parasites would ever allow.

Ryan also brought a lot of middle-class workers down to Rapture. They were required to build the city in the first place. But since Rapture was born on a philosophy that rejects supporting others, there was no support system for these people once their jobs were completed. The result was a fairly large population of people left destitute and expected to fend for themselves.

Still, for years it worked as Ryan imagined. Rapture experienced unparalleled economic and scientific progress.

The most important advance was made by Brigid Tenenbaum, a brilliant scientist who saw Rapture as an opportunity for redemption after her participation in horrible experiments in Nazi Germany. She discovered a sea slug that excreted a substance that held the secret to immense amounts of genetic alteration. But even in Rapture, a society based on no scientific restrictions, Brigid struggled to find funding until she met Frank Fontaine, who agreed to fund her research if he kept all the profits from the venture.

The research went better than anyone had hoped. In short order, Tenenbaum's discoveries cured diseases and allowed the genetic code of a species to be altered in amazing ways, even providing them with superhuman abilities. Seen as a rebirth for humanity, this substance that Brigid created was named ADAM.

Later, it was discovered that when this sea slug was placed in the stomach of a human host, it produced considerably more, twenty to thirty times more ADAM. Inexplicably, and unfortunately, the only hosts for these grotesque sea slugs were young girls.

So, being the ruthless businessman he was, Fontaine opened the Fontaine's Little Sisters Orphanage, advertising it as a haven for impoverished families to send their young girls for better care than they could provide on their own.

Of course, the orphanage was just a front for producing ADAM. The girls sent there would have the slug implanted in them in secret. Tenenbaum was disturbed by this and wanted to keep the hosts in a vegetative state, thinking that was better than the alternative, but in another cruel twist of fate for the girls, the slugs only seemed to work when the host was awake and active.

With a steady supply of ADAM, Fontaine Futuristics began to mass-produce and distribute large quantities of intravenous cocktails called plasmids.

At first, Ryan praised Fontaine for his success. After all, through his own ingenuity and investments, he'd not only improved the human condition, but he had also amassed large amounts of wealth. But eventually, Ryan learned that Fontaine was smuggling plasmids to the surface in exchange for Bibles and other religious items for the homesick citizens of Rapture. Determined that Rapture would be totally independent of the old world, Ryan tried to disband the smuggling ring, and Fontaine was killed in a shoot-out with Ryan's men. Leaving Ryan in charge of Fontaine Futuristics and the Little Sisters.

Soon the demand for ADAM grew faster than the Little Sisters could provide, so Ryan went to his preferred doctor, Yi Suchong, who invented the Big Daddies. They were basically lobotomized criminals who were conditioned to protect the Little Sisters, then placed in weaponized suits of armor. The Little Sisters were trained to extract ADAM from dead bodies found around Rapture, effectively recycling the stuff, and the Big Daddies would follow them around obediently to protect them.

At this point, it's pretty safe to say that Rapture had gotten pretty messed up. And while this is a *lot* of info, there is still so much more that I'm leaving behind. Really, the depth of this game and the amount of work that went into the backstory is . . . well, it's overwhelming.

But, to make things worse, this whole takeover of Fontaine Futuristics did not sit well with the people of Rapture. Fontaine was well loved, while Ryan was simply revered. And eventually someone came along to stir things up a little more, a man known as Atlas.

Remember when I mentioned the working-class people who were left to fend for themselves after building Rapture? Well, those people were pretty easy to rile up. It didn't take Atlas long to incite a civil war. Chaos erupted, and people took advantage of the plasmids to join the fight. They abused the plasmids to a point where they began to lose their minds, splicing their personalities into so many pieces that eventually they became genetically modified mutants known as . . . you guessed it, the Splicers.

In the end, the only way for Ryan to stop the war was to go against his own core belief in free will. To preserve his own freedom, he allowed Suchong to embed a form of mind control into the plasmids the Splicers were using. Ryan regained control of Rapture just as our un-spliced hero, Jack, happened upon his front door.

Eventually Jack finds his way to where Ryan is holed up. But here's where things go from odd to mind-blowing. Also, here's your parachute moment. You can know all this stuff and still play the game without knowing what is considered by many, myself included, as one of the best twists in storytelling *ever*.

You still with me?

Are you sure?

Before Jack walks into Ryan's actual office, he comes across a room with the words WOULD YOU KINDLY painted sloppily over a bunch of photographs, small notes, and random papers tacked to a wall. It looks like the work of a madman, and as he studies it, he sees familiar faces as well as two new audio diaries. The first audio recording seems fairly straightforward as it recounts the successful results of an experiment concerning advanced human growth rates, but the other is not quite so academic.

BioShock © 2K Games

The second audio diary opens with the sound of a puppy playing, then the voice Jack has come to recognize as Yi Suchong speaking to a little child. He remarks on how cute the puppy is, and the child agrees. It yips as he plays with it, and Jack can imagine it licking the boy's rosy cheeks as he grins at his new pet. Then Suchong asks the child to break its neck. The boy starts crying, begging to not be asked to do it. With determination in his broken voice, he says he won't. Suchong asks again, this time using the phrase "Would you kindly break the puppy's neck?" The boy cries, still begging not to do it as the puppy yelps, then his voice fades away.

This evocative recording reverberates in Jack's mind as he stares at the wall with the same words WOULD YOU KINDLY painted hastily in red. After regretting making this disturbing discovery, he moves forward into the office of Andrew Ryan. Inside, he finds Ryan putting golf balls on a narrow green carpet. He's not shocked to see Jack, nor is he afraid of what he'll do to him. He isn't, because he already knows. The wheels have been set in motion, and there is nothing anyone can do about it. But before Jack does what he's come to do, Ryan takes the time to change his world.

Ryan explains that things are not what they seem. You, as Jack, have memories of being raised on a farm by a loving family. And you, as you *and* Jack, have memories of sitting in a plane and a plane crash. And as you remember these things, we experience flashbacks of Jack's actually being raised in Rapture by doctors. Ryan asks what the difference is between a man and a slave, then he gives you the answer. A man chooses, a slave obeys. He reminds Jack of the phrase *would you kindly* once again, and the flashbacks return. Jack hears the phrase repeated as he injects the first vial of plasmids at the beginning of the game. Remember that moment? It's the one I questioned at the beginning and now we see why this wasn't a choice for the player. Jack hears the phrase again as he begins to follow Atlas's commands. Then again and again. Each time Jack made a decision in the game, it followed those three words: would you kindly. This often took place in cut scenes, or short moments where the game took control from the player. It's something we've become so accustomed to in games that it was easy to overlook as a simple storytelling mechanic, but in *BioShock*, it is so much more. They used this gaming mechanic to express what free will is, or perhaps even accurately, the lack of free will.

Your controller (or keyboard and mouse) becomes useless as Andrew Ryan demonstrates the power of the command. He tells Jack, "Would you kindly sit?" and Jack sits. Stand and he stands. Run and he runs. Turn around, and he turns around.

Ryan hands Jack the golf club, knowing Atlas has already asked, "Would you kindly find Ryan and finish him." It is inevitable. From the moment he walked into the room, Andrew Ryan knew he was already gone, but he wanted Jack to perform the action knowing that he was a slave. Jack proceeds, or rather, the game proceeds, to take Ryan's life, beating him to death with the golf club.

In seconds, Atlas is back in your ear, barking more orders with his powerful phrase. Jack turns off the self-destruct sequence, saving the city as he was commanded. Knowing Jack's done all he could for him, Atlas has more secrets to tell. He begins to lose control, laughing maniacally, as he tells Jack there is no Atlas. His name is Frank Fontaine, and people wrongly assumed he was dead after a shoot-out. If you've played the game, at this moment, you can feel the significance of this reveal. All along you've been following the orders of the most wanted enemy in the world of Rapture.

A new set of audio diaries is revealed, and we learn even more of Jack's true story. We learn of a woman, Jasmine Jolene, who was a chorus girl and dancer in Rapture. She was a favorite of Ryan's, and eventually she got pregnant with his child. Afraid to tell him, she confessed the news to a friend, but Fontaine, having bugged her room, found out and took action. At his request, Tenenbaum offers to remove her baby in exchange for a large sum of money and tells her that Ryan will never be the wiser. Jasmine accepts the offer and, suspecting no greater plot, moves on with her life below the sea.

Unfortunately for her, Ryan found out about it and murdered Jasmine in a fit of rage. I found this completely out of character for Ryan. Or perhaps outside of his philosophy. What Jasmine did in giving up the baby to benefit herself and only herself fits squarely within the objectivist ideology. Ryan, who believes that giving in to emotions is a weakness, shows us that even though he believes fully in his ideals, he is unable to control even himself. Hypocritical of the way he's treated others, including those in his city? Yes. Understandable? Well, not really. It's further than any of *us* would go, but then again, that's part of Ryan's character, too. Extremes are his modus operandi.

At this point, Yi Suchong returns to the backstory. The baby boy survived and was experimented on, making him stronger and faster than the average person. But Suchong's specialty was psychological conditioning, as he proved by programming the Little Sisters, the Big Daddies, and the Splicers. And he practiced his skills on the boy as he aged, conditioning him to respond uncontrollably to the phrase *would you kindly.*

Sometime before faking his own death in the shoot-out, Fontaine smuggled the child out of Rapture as a sleeper agent, implanting fake memories of his family and life on the surface. When Ryan defeated Atlas's army of Splicers, Fontaine activated his backup plan. Thus the package with the large red bow on it in the opening sequence. The things we were unable to read in the beginning are now made clear as we watch a series of flashback cut scenes. We learn that it says "would you kindly not open this package until" followed by some coordinates that brought Jack, and the plane of innocent bystanders, to the lighthouse where the crash took place. Oh, and that "stronger than others" thing is also the reason Jack was the only survivor of the plane crash. As Jack, you're nearly indestructible, and Atlas knew this all along.

Jack learns that he is the son of the man he just killed and that he's been operating against his will at the commands of Atlas (Frank Fontaine) all along.

Okay, if you haven't played this, I know what you're thinking here. Sure, it's a twist, and you didn't see it coming, but how does *that* have impact? Why do I claim it is the best plot twist in gaming? Well, there's a lot to unpack here. What the developers did here as a commentary on gameplay itself is quite brilliant.

In *BioShock*, especially as a first-person game, we get the impression that the choices we make as we play are under our control. From the small, below-the-neck verb decisions like aiming, running, jumping, etc., to the larger decisions like navigation, which plasmid weapons to choose, and which audio diaries to listen to. And then, of course, there are the moral decisions the game offers, the above-the-neck verb decisions, like the choice to harvest or rescue. With this twist, *BioShock* makes you question if any of these decisions are yours to make in the first place or if the games we play direct outcomes for us from the start.

As we explore the world and play the game, we feel as if we understand the rules and have agency inside the city of Rapture, but in reality, we have nothing of the sort. It is so brilliant because not only is it a fantastic twist to the narrative, but it also used us and our expectations of how video games work to have us blindly (or kindly) follow the rules the game set before us. In fact, I'd dare say we enjoy doing so.

And this plot twist hits so hard because while you're wrestling with the idea that Jack is actually the son of Ryan and that he is part of Fontaine's evil plans in the narrative, *you* have also been played by the game.

It's taken us some time to get here, but hopefully now you understand why I was worried about spoiling the heck out of those who haven't played the game. And there are still more questions to ask. What really is being said by the moral choices in the game, and what happens if you chose to rescue the Little Sisters? Or worse, what happens if you don't? Because while this is the end of the chapter, it isn't the end of the game. That's right, I'm leaving a bit more for you to explore. The choices you've made along the way *do* affect how the game ends. It's the twist after the twist. You learn that you've been under someone else's control all along, only to discover that perhaps agency, choice, your own personal moral decisions are important after all. What does this say about objectivism? What does this say about us?

Good questions, and there are so many more. But the only one I have left is this: Would you kindly play through this storytelling masterpiece? Dive deep below the mid-Atlantic, in search of more answers within the dark and horrific hallways of Rapture. You will return to the surface changed.

BOOK REPORT:

Psychonauts

Psychonauts © Double Fine Productions

INITIAL RELEASE DATE AND PLATFORM:

April 2005 for Xbox, PlayStation 2, Windows PC

WHERE ELSE CAN IT BE FOUND?

The game can pretty easily be found on Steam. It was also re-released in 2016 for the PlayStation 4, and it can be found today on all current platforms.

CATEGORY:

Linear Narrative, Platforming Adventure

MAIN CHARACTERS:

Razputin (Raz) Aquato, a ten-year-old superpsychic packed with courage and heart, and the protagonist of the story

Lili Zanotto, a powerful psychic and serial truant who would rather garden than go to class. She is the daughter of the grand head of the Psychonauts and a veteran at Whispering Rock Psychic Summer Camp.

Dr. Caligosto Loboto, D.D.S., an insane ex-dentist and freelancing scientist who serves as one of the antagonists of *Psychonauts*

SETTING:

Psychonauts is set in the fictional Whispering Rock Psychic Summer Camp.

Centuries ago, the area was hit by a meteor made of psitanium, an element that can grant psychic powers or strengthen existing powers. Such as bears with the ability to attack with telekinetic claws, cougars with pyrokinesis, and rats with confusion gas, but it wasn't just the animals that were affected. The humans paid a toll as well.

Soon, an asylum had to be built for the afflicted humans, but within fifteen years, the asylum had more residents than the town itself. After the director of the asylum fell to disaster, leaving the place without the care it needed to continue, the government relocated the inhabitants that remained, then proceeded to flood the crater the psitanium meteor created, apparently to prevent things from going awry again, creating what is now Lake Oblongata.

However, the government secretly took advantage of the psitanium deposit to set up a training camp for psychonauts, a group of agents gifted with psychic abilities. The training ground was disguised as a summer camp for young children, but in reality, the place was there to teach the children to hone their abilities and to train them to become psychonauts themselves.

Story Summary:

Psychonauts is the story of Rasputin (Raz) Aquato, a young psychic who runs away from the circus to sneak into Whispering Rock.

There, he quickly learns that someone is stealing the brains of the other campers. Tracking the source of this scheme, Raz finds himself quite literally getting into the heads of a variety of other characters on his quest to save the world.

What Did You Think of This Story?

The story, which starts with an inversion of the usual "run away to join the circus" trope, is not the only memorable thing about this game. The platforming aspect of *Psychonauts* is filled with strange and nonsensical architecture, and sometimes is actually quite hard.

But what really makes it stand out is the level of detail. All the dialogue is voiced, and no matter what item or ability Raz uses, or what scenario he pulls a character into, there's probably a unique reaction programmed in. And more than that, most of the characters have intricate side plots, with hidden conversations Raz can eavesdrop on and individual cut scenes for you to discover.

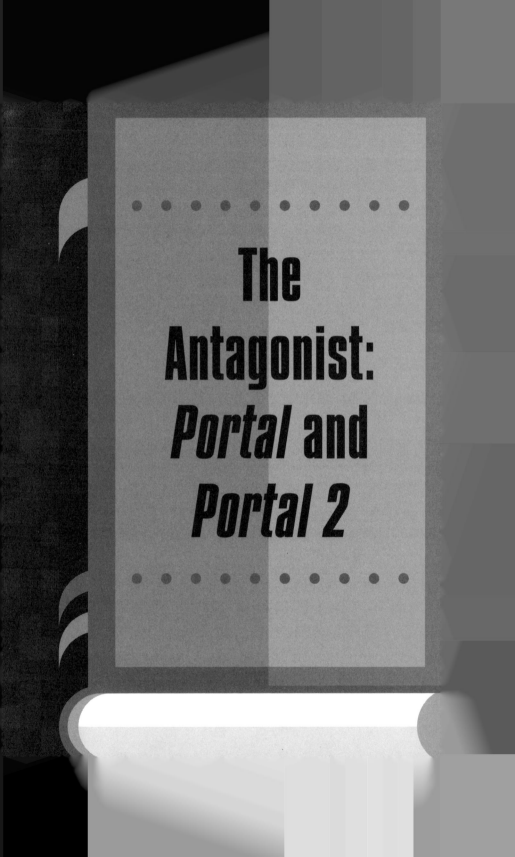

The Antagonist: *Portal* and *Portal 2*

One of the things I most enjoy about story is the conflict between the protagonist and the antagonist. Which, as you can imagine, can present a problem when the protagonist is silent.

I KNOW, I KNOW. I JUST SPENT BASICALLY AN ENTIRE chapter talking about how great it is that silent protagonists allow you to become the character. But that is also one of their greatest weaknesses. Let's face it, not all of us lead lives as interesting as, say, Nathan Drake, so when we are expected to bring our own experiences to a character . . . well, a silent protagonist is almost always a bit of a blank slate.

For a silent protagonist to work, the surrounding elements of the game have to be spectacular. And the *Portal* games really deliver on this in one of the most amazing and compelling manners ever, with GLaDOS, the computer voice that guides our silent protagonist Chell.

While *Portal* starts off slow, with very little explanation, the game cleverly reveals one of the most talked-about lores in video game history. We learn that in 1947, Aperture Science Enrichment Center was created to make shower curtains for the US military.

The owner, Cave Johnson, fell ill thanks to his secret production of a conversion gel made from lunar rocks, prompting him to produce a three-tiered research program to ensure the longevity of his company. First, the Heimlich Counter-Maneuver. Second, the Take-A-Wish Foundation. And third, the Portal Project, which included the making of the Aperture Science Handheld Portal Device, aka the portal gun. The last was endlessly funded by the Senate, and Johnson went on to . . . well, die.

Fast-forward many years later, when an AI research assistant known as "Genetic Lifeform and Disk Operating System"—aka GLaDOS—is activated on the Enrichment Center's first Bring Your Daughter to Work Day. After releasing a neurotoxin, locking everyone inside, and taking over the facility, GLaDOS is equipped with a morality core to keep her murderous impulses in line. The morality core is a failure, and thus the Aperture test chambers were created for GLaDOS's enjoyment.

The remaining employees were forced to further develop and test the Portal Project using the nifty portal guns. It's unknown how long those poor souls lasted in the nearly abandoned Enrichment Center, but eventually GLaDOS finds herself with only one test subject left, Chell, who GLaDOS wakes up from her stasis bed. GLaDOS tells Chell she's trapped in the Enrichment Center and must make her way through the test chambers . . . and so the adventure that is *Portal* begins.

As you use the portal gun to make your way out of the Enrichment Center, GLaDOS is there every step of the way. She provides somewhat useful hints and somewhat misleading directions. The game is puzzle platforming played in first person, set in full 3D space, which would be enough of a mind-bender on its own, but with GLaDOS promising Chell cake for solving puzzles and nearly killing her at every turn, the game turns into a pyscho-thriller, pseudohumor romp in a bizarre sci-fi setting that will stick with you for years.

GLaDOS in Portal © Valve

In the end of *Portal*, we discover that GLaDOS wasn't only a bit confused at times, she was downright evil, and she takes great joy in killing people within the environment she controls. And not only that, the cake was a lie all along. Rude.

GLaDOS returns in *Portal 2*, as we play as Chell, a character we still barely know. After what GLaDOS did in the first game, it's impossible for us to trust her again, or so it would seem. But in a matter of a few hours, the brilliant writing and voice acting of GLaDOS shines through, and we begin to slowly build up a relationship with her.

And in *Portal 2*, GLaDOS shifts from being the antagonist in the first game to the deuteragonist, the second in importance to you, the protagonist in the game.

But the only way to have dual protagonists in this story and maintain the external conflict, or the plot, is by introducing a new antagonist to work against Chell (you) and GLaDOS. Enter Wheatley, the Intelligence Dampening Sphere, voiced by British comedian and writer Stephen Merchant. If you know his work, you can probably imagine how brilliant his voice acting is in this game, and believe me, he delivers one of the most dangerously funny and unexpected performances as he voices the little floating ball.

The relationship between Chell and GLaDOS evolves in an extremely believable way. This slow relationship based on rebuilding of trust, and with the addition of Wheatley, is the reason this story is so outstanding. Both have been bamboozled by Wheatley and have to work together to stop him from destroying the facility. After being cast down much farther into the earth than they already were, GLaDOS is in a state of vulnerability, something she has never been in up until this point. The game makes sure you know this by having various birds appear that spook the living hell out of Potato GLaDOS. (Yes, that's a thing. You know if you know, and if you don't, wait until you find out.) I found her fall from towering villain to helpless damsel to be interesting. It is what gave GLaDOS the perspective to regain her most human persona.

I know this sounds odd and a bit difficult to follow, but that's kind of how the game is. Odd and a bit difficult to follow. This kind of setup works wonders because it effectively gives the player the best of both worlds. As we play, we can put ourselves in the character's headspace and feel as though GLaDOS is really talking to us.

We discover who GLaDOS used to be, but not only do *we* learn this, GLaDOS learns it along with us, making us feel invested in her story. She's just so wickedly charming that we find ourselves enamored with her as she grows and decides to alter the AI inside the game, which is the first step in resolving a complicated conflict between Chell, the silent protagonist, and GLaDOS.

Potato GLaDOS in Portal 2 © Valve

The antagonists in these two *Portal* games take what could be a very forgettable protagonist (silent to boot) and make this story beyond memorable. They add danger and mistrust, color and fear, humor and humanity, all packed into two cold and lifeless AI drive robots with enough heart to make us feel.

This game is brilliant. It's so much fun to play, and the story is equal parts charming, thrilling, and hilarious. It really is something that should be played, and if you haven't had a chance, add it to your wish list on Steam. You'll be glad you did.

BOOK REPORT:

Half-Life 2

Half-Life 2 © Valve

INITIAL RELEASE DATE AND PLATFORM:

2004 for PC by way of Steam first, then released shortly after on DVD in stores around the globe

WHERE ELSE CAN IT BE FOUND?

Since then, *Half-Life 2* has been packaged with other Valve hits in the popular release called Orange Box. It is also easy to find today on Steam for Windows PC and Mac OS, as well as on the Xbox, Xbox 360, PlayStation 3, Linux, and Android. Basically, it's everywhere.

CATEGORY:

Linear Narrative, First-Person Shooter

MAIN CHARACTERS:

Gordon Freeman, the playable character and silent protagonist of the story

The G-Man, the overarching antagonist of the *Half-Life* series, although his true identity and motives remain unexplained

Alyx Vance, the deuteragonist of *Half-Life*. The closest thing to an ally Freeman has and a prominent figure in the Resistance campaign against the rule of the Combine.

SETTING:

In a gray environment in Eastern Europe, nestled in the quiet town of White Forest, you can't help but notice the Soviet-era ICBM silo and factory-like buildings that dot the landscape. You play in City 17, the fictional area that looks oddly familiar and believable but at the same time off-putting and unwelcoming, creating the exact mood the developers were after for *Half-Life 2*.

STORY SUMMARY:

Following Valve Software Corporation's *Half-Life* (released in 1998), *Half-Life 2* takes players outside of the Black Mesa research corporation and into City 17, where the alien force known as the Combine have taken over Earth in part of their hopes of intergalactic domination. Former Black Mesa scientist Gordon Freeman is forcibly thrust into the now dystopian planet to secure the survival of the ever-so-diminishing human species. With the help of such allies as Alyx Vance, other former Black Mesa scientists, and more, it is up to Dr. Freeman to stop the Combine and once again save the world.

WHAT DID YOU THINK OF THIS STORY?

The exterior conflict and gunplay in this game are top-notch. Jump scares abound, and the AI was way ahead of its time. But beyond the compelling dystopian story and the cold concrete environments contrasted with blood-covered, toothy aliens, once again, a huge part of the appeal of this story is the silent protagonist. This game takes first person to a whole new level, by forcing you to put yourself in Gordon Freeman's shoes and think your way through the dialogue as a participant. It was the inner conflict, the mysterious G-Man, and the slow realization that not only do you need to put an end to the chaos, but you had a hand in creating the mess in the first place that really makes this game shine.

Red Dead Redemption II

In Medias Res (Adv.) (Latin)
In the middle of things.

THE DUTCH BOYS GANG IS ON THE RUN AFTER A heist gone sour in the Wild West town of Blackwater. Bounty hunters, special agents, and the Pinkertons are hot on their trail. In a desperate move, the charismatic leader, Dutch van der Linde, guides his freezing, starving people through the wintry Grizzlies mountain pass. The gambit pays off, and they shake the law. But their troubles are far from over. They must survive a blizzard in a ramshackle ghost town.

Instead of a loosely knit cluster of hard-bitten, dusty men smoking cigarettes and sleeping with a revolver and one eye open, Dutch's gang looks more like a diverse orphan family. There are a dozen men and women, young and old, black and white, and even a child. They appear poor and innocent, and it's hard not to sympathize with them.

Dutch, with weight in his gravelly voice, manages to choke out an emotional speech to the downtrodden with the rhetoric of a magnetic cult leader. Despite losing beloved gang members in the recently botched ferry robbery, and being chased through the perilous mountains, he rouses his troops by reminding them they've only made it as far as they have by sticking with him. He begs them to stay together a little while longer and concludes his speech by promising to lead them west, to a promised land, away from the outstretched arm of the law. His followers are so tired, but they would leave heaven if it meant joining Dutch in hell. With a swish of his cloak, Dutch orders Arthur Morgan, his right-hand man, surrogate son, and the protagonist of the story, to ride out with him into the dark and stormy night.

Now that is how you hook an audience!

Red Dead Redemption II © Rockstar Games

Red Dead Redemption II is a linear branching narrative, open-world game set in 1899 that tells a Wild West story through the eyes of Arthur Morgan, longtime member of the infamous criminal outfit the Dutch Boys. Arthur laments the early death of his glory days as an outlaw, cut short by wicked industry and civilization, which is an idea that has been drilled into his head by Dutch over many years. He isn't the typical goody-two-shoes sheriff type seen in other Western stories, and yet he is still one of the most beloved protagonists in video games. There is so much to be said about the numerous achievements of this massive game, but my focus is going to be primarily on Arthur's story.

In my opinion, three major contributing factors make *Red Dead Redemption II* one of the greatest stories ever played: The first is the bond between Arthur Morgan and Dutch van der Linde. Of all the numerous characters we are introduced to, this is the relationship that generates the most conflict in Arthur's soul. The second is Arthur's backstory, and the third is the mysterious Blackwater incident. These three elements give us context into who Arthur was, which makes the contrast of who he will become in the end even more astounding.

Red Dead Redemption II starts *in medias res*, a Latin phrase meaning "into the middle of things." The idea behind *in medias res* is that it hurries the audience into the action and demands that they take notice. People often interpret this to mean the beginning of a captivating story has to be action-packed with lots of moving parts and characters you don't fully understand until it is explained later. But that is only partially true.

Stories need plot, regardless if they start at the beginning or in the middle of things. But not only must the first event in a story be attention-grabbing, it must also change the characters in the story. It is also true that there must be some significant event, the inciting incident, to kick the main plot into motion, otherwise there never would be a story. An inciting incident with no consideration of who the characters were before that moment and why the event is significant to them is just action without purpose. So what's important isn't that the audience is thrown into the middle of the action, it's that they are thrown into the middle of the story.

In this case, the inciting incident of *Red Dead Redemption II* is the botched ferry robbery at Blackwater, which results in the law placing a dead-or-alive bounty on the Dutch Boys. Blackwater is the explanation as to why the gang is traveling through the mountains in the first place. More important, Blackwater is the event that causes Arthur to change. Interestingly, though, the game begins with the gang escaping through the mountains during a snowstorm and not with the Blackwater incident. So, although it is part of the plot, players never experience what happened there.

Red Dead Redemption II is bold in going so far as to never allow you to play, or even see, the inciting incident. Some of the details of what happened at Blackwater are told through parts of the game that are separate from the main story missions altogether. The same goes for some of Arthur's personal backstory. In *Red Dead Redemption II*, we learn more about Arthur's past and the Blackwater event by talking with gang members at camp over a bowl of stew; by reading Arthur's journal, which he periodically updates; by buying and reading the newspaper; or by completing side quests. If you don't stumble upon those details, or go out of your way to find them, you might never discover them. And, depending on your point of view, they can be crucial to totally understanding Arthur's internal dilemma throughout the game.

In a novel, every word printed in the physical book is identical to every other copy. If you read every word, then you have experienced everything the author intended you to. In *Red Dead Redemption II*, the creators make elements of the story optional, with no guarantee that players will find them. I guess this method would be the equivalent of locking a chapter of a book and giving readers all the clues to unlock it, but never explicitly telling them how to do so. You could argue that optional storytelling is a strength, or a weakness. But either way, you have to admit that this sets video games apart from books, movies, and comics.

To truly understand how the incident at Blackwater changed Arthur, I had to look back to when Arthur and Dutch first met, decades before the story started. And keep in mind that, similar to *BioShock*, much of this information isn't in the main plot. Instead, I often had to search for it in side quests and other optional material.

There are times in real life where the challenges we deal with on a daily basis stem from an event in our past that is too difficult to cope with, so we ignore it because it's the easiest short-term solution. But that's precisely the problem, it's just short-term. Eventually the reverberations appear louder, in unexpected ways, to get our attention, and there will be experiences that remind us of our pain and bring them to the forefront. For Arthur Morgan, that painful reminder occurred at Blackwater.

At eleven years old, Arthur watched his father, a two-bit thief convicted of larceny, hang. Angry and confused at the world, the boy was on his own until age thirteen, when he was picked up by Dutch van der Linde and Hosea Matthews. The three became founding members of the Dutch Boys gang.

It's hard to say whether Dutch, who became a sort of father figure to the teen, took on Arthur for altruistic reasons or not, but regardless of his motivation, their relationship resulted in Arthur's adopting Dutch's ideals and values, in other words, an outlaw code. To live free from the tyranny of government, to never harm the innocent and only rob the deserving, and that revenge is a fool's game.

Years later, Arthur met a waitress outside of the gang named Eliza, and after a quick affair, they had a son named Isaac. Arthur, a good and humble person at his core, wanted to do right by them, even if he had some distorted ideas about honesty because of his line of work.

Living the life of an outlaw pulled Arthur away from his home with Eliza often, and after a stint on the trail, he returned one day to find two small crosses outside. The innocent mother and child were murdered in their own home by robbers, all for a measly ten dollars. The experience deeply wounded Arthur and called his own morality into question. Could he live with himself being a criminal in his own right? If he continued down that path, would he see himself one day become the same as the men who killed his family?

Dutch comforted Arthur and encouraged his distraught surrogate son to hold fast to another line in his outlaw code: There is nothing worse than being a murderer *for no good reason.*

Arthur took his advice, and it's hard to blame him. After all, if he forsook Dutch and the gang, he would be an orphan again. It's understandable that he wouldn't abandon the only family he has left, even if it meant burying the pain of Eliza and Isaac's deaths. Unfortunately for our protagonist, the pain never went away. Deep down, he knew that by remaining an outlaw, he was not honoring his deceased family's memory, and living contrary to his core moral compass filled him with self-loathing over the years. But at least Arthur could dam the pain as long as Dutch kept his word. That all changed at Blackwater when Dutch, and a new shady member of the gang, Micah Bell, decided, with little planning, to rob a ferry in the port city. After an argument of whether to try to pull off the job, Dutch waited until Arthur was away on another job to attempt the risky robbery, and things went horribly wrong.

Members of the gang were captured, some died, and the few that escaped with their lives had no spoils to show for their troubles. But the thing that caused the most turmoil for Arthur was the murder of an innocent woman. A bystander named Heidi McCourt.

Heidi's murder is a direct contradiction to everything Dutch has preached. And as soon as Arthur learns about it, he begins to lose faith in his hero, the man who gave his word they were better than the robbers who killed Arthur's family. As soon as Dutch broke his vow, the temporary dam that poorly held back Arthur's heartache broke, too, and he had to relive the pain of losing Eliza and Isaac once more.

From the opening scene, we can sense the growing distrust Arthur has in his leader. And Dutch can see it, too. They both know why Arthur has lost his faith in him, but neither will come right out and say it. Instead, Dutch accuses Arthur of undermining and challenging his authority, and Arthur tries to constantly reaffirm his loyalty to Dutch, in word and deed. But Dutch's feeble attempts to seal the Pandora's box he split open when he murdered Heidi McCourt are all in vain. He can't pretend to be something he's not any longer. Dutch is no different from the men who killed Eliza and Isaac, and that realization reminds Arthur of his worst fear, that he is just like them, too.

This is the major source of internal conflict that keeps us hooked. When we understand the powerful forces that drive Arthur to seek redemption for failing the memory of Eliza and Isaac for so many years and contrast it with his desire to make Dutch proud, we can't put the controller down until the resolution. And it only gets harder for Arthur the further Dutch descends into moral depravity.

In many ways, the events at Blackwater are a harbinger of things to come. Arthur isn't alone in his relationship with Dutch. Over the years, Dutch has cleverly sought out potential gang members who were at one point in need of saving. Nearly every member was on the brink of losing themselves when Dutch, a valiant, well-spoken, well-dressed, well-to-do man, gave them a purpose and added them to his family, as he so often calls the gang.

But the problem with Dutch is that although he is a very skilled manipulator, he is an awful criminal. Time and time again, he promises his ardent followers one last big haul, but he fails. Especially when he doesn't listen to Hosea's sage advice.

Dutch responds to his constant failures by becoming even more erratic, seemingly abandoning his lifelong rhetoric that he's protecting his family by putting their lives in greater danger with his increasingly harebrained schemes. This careless treatment of people, as if they were toy soldiers for Dutch to play with, widens the gap between him and Arthur as these problems become more pronounced.

Arthur's initial torment of losing his family and then seeing how Dutch manipulates people by coming to their rescue and demanding lifelong loyalty work in tandem to fuel Arthur's motivation to change. Arthur isn't proud of the way he's lived, but simply having the right motivation to change isn't enough. He doesn't feel safe leaving behind his criminal life with Dutch. Sure, the truth he learns about Dutch in Blackwater is the event that kicks things off, but the transition from who Arthur was to who he becomes starts with a man he doesn't even know until he's sent to collect a debt: Thomas Downes.

The first town the gang settled in after hiding away in the mountains was Valentine. It's small, making it a popular waypoint for people on the run. There's a saloon, a general store, and a bank. Thomas Downes was the town crier, a good man who advocated for the less fortunate by raising charitable donations, until he finds himself caught in an all-too-familiar struggle, compiling significant debts on his ranch as he tries to make ends meet. He was the perfect victim for Leopold Strauss, accountant and moneylender of the Dutch Boys, who gave Mr. Downes an offer he couldn't refuse. Desperate to provide for his wife and son, Mr. Downes accepted the loan without a plan on how to pay off the debt in time. Arthur was sent in Leopold Strauss's place to retrieve Mr. Downes's payment and to intimidate him, if necessary. A job Arthur begrudgingly excels at.

Arthur finds the destitute farmer, coughing loudly and struggling to tend to a failing garden on a tiny plot of land. Arthur demands the money, but the ill man has no way to pay it. Arthur beats him bloody in front of his family until he confesses that they already owe more than the house is worth and that the ranch has no potential income. There isn't a scrap Arthur can take back to the gang to compensate for their loss. In a fit, Arthur stomps off, with nothing more than a face full of blood, coughed up by the feeble man. He shouts behind him, telling Downes to have the money before his next visit.

Arthur returns a couple of weeks later to find that Thomas died because of complications brought on by the assault. Dispassionately, Arthur tries to explain away his guilt to Thomas's wife, Edith Downes, by justifying that they live in a world of fury. Her husband was bound to die anyway, regardless of his interference. But the freshly widowed woman sees right through Arthur and accuses him of murdering Thomas. Despite their hardship, the Downes family somehow found a way to pay off their debt to the Dutch Boys. Arthur recovers the money and returns to camp.

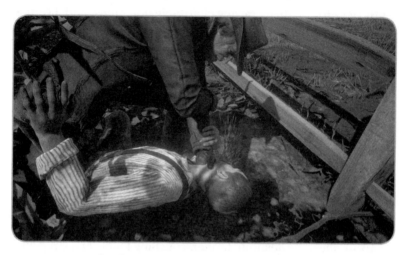

Red Dead Redemption II © Rockstar Games

Arthur has always hated usury, the practice of lending money and expecting an unreasonable return, because it has usually meant he had to strong-arm desperate people who were forced to make very difficult decisions. Deep down, he can empathize with them, but he tries his darndest to harden those emotions. To Arthur, it feels contrary to the gang's values, but Dutch convinced him it was a necessary evil. Arthur relies often on Dutch to ease his troubled conscience. If he didn't, Arthur would have to address the guilt he feels dishonoring his family's memory, and that would mean making an uncomfortable, drastic change in lifestyle. But the Downes family was by far the most depressing of all the gang's clients, and although Arthur puts on a rough exterior, it is obvious it bothered him.

Arthur writes in his journal how conflicted he feels about his experience with the Downes family. He describes a raging conflict in his soul, and that he doesn't know if what he's doing is right or wrong. This indicates Arthur is beginning to snap out of the years-long brainwashing induced by Dutch and is considering if he can live with the effects his choices have on people.

The gameplay reflects Arthur's internal dialogue by introducing the honor scale shortly after the Downes murder. The honor scale is a bar at the bottom of the screen that shows how good or evil Arthur is. If you make a bad choice, the scale skews left; if you make a good one, it skews right. This mechanic is neat because it actually has a purpose unrelated to gameplay. It represents his inner struggle. Instead of thoughtlessly killing and robbing in the name of the outlaw code, he's weighing the implications of what his bad decisions have on his soul. Depending on your morality at the end of the game, you will get a different outcome. The biggest difference between the different endings is whether Arthur believes he finds the titular redemption.

The tipping point in Arthur's journey happens when he learns that while beating Thomas Downes, he caught Thomas's tuberculosis, a fatal disease. Weeks of dealing with the horrible sickness brings Arthur to his lowest point. Despite Dutch's influence, he can finally be totally truthful about who he feels he is. Being at death's door forces Arthur to reflect honestly on who he has become and regret the decisions he's made. While Arthur is struggling with his illness, Dutch drags him along on increasingly desperate, improvised schemes. Arthur questions Dutch's sanity, and Dutch in response shuts Arthur out of his inner circle, replacing him and other sentimental gang members with suspicious guns for hire.

Not knowing how to feel about his newfound freedom from Dutch's rule, Arthur goes out of his way to help return a stolen cross to a nunnery. Afterward, Sister Calderón, a kindly spirit, graciously invites him inside for some food. A little uncomfortable, having never been much of a religious person, he declines. Sister Calderón tells Arthur he is a good man because he helped someone in need when he didn't have to. The remark actually makes the sickly man chuckle at the incredulity of it. Him? A good man? She had no idea who she was talking to. But instead of lecturing her, he goes on his way with the touch of a smile on his face.

You might be wondering why Arthur would do this? Most of his life has been spent in pursuit of skillfully pulling the wool over a sad sap's eyes long enough to rob them blind or to shoot 'em dead. Why would Arthur go out of his way to help someone if he had nothing to gain from it? In a later conversation with Sister Calderón, we'll see evidence that Arthur had at this point totally abandoned the paradigm Dutch instilled in him since his youth. The outlaw code didn't mean anything to him anymore because its greatest proponent never truly believed in it in the first place. If you're playing for redemption here, really following the path that will lead toward Arthur's trying to make up for the mistakes in his life, then you experience along with Arthur the realization that these decisions were his own all along, causing him true remorse for the wicked life he led. Not only for all the robbing and the killing, but I think he felt especially guilty about the hypocrisy. About willfully soiling the memory of Eliza and Isaac for so many years and denying that he knew it was wrong all along.

This brief interaction with Sister Calderón kicks off a series of events where Arthur decides to defy Dutch's commands in order to help those in need. Maybe he had a change of heart because he was encouraged by her insistence that he was a good man. Or maybe when his life felt darkest, choosing to be charitable instead of destructive made him feel good. We don't know why for sure. But for whatever reason, Arthur has the courage to stand up to Dutch, the man he owed his life to, the person he feared the most.

Arthur's attention turns to members of the gang Dutch once professed to provide for and protect. One family in particular, Abigail and John Marston, and their little boy, Jack, stands out to Arthur as something that is still worth fighting for.

One of the greatest indicators of Arthur's character development is a conversation he has with Sister Calderón just a few days after meeting her.

Arthur finds Sister Calderón waiting at the train station, on her way to serve a mission in Mexico. He greets her amicably and then doubles over in a fit of coughing. He is reaching the terminal stages of his sickness, and the concerned sister has to help him take a seat to catch his breath.

Red Dead Redemption II © Rockstar Games

He didn't plan on seeing her again, but he quickly makes it obvious that he is searching for something inside their conversation. In a rare moment of vulnerability, he spills the beans to Sister Calderón. He tells her, "I got TB. I got it from beatin' a man to death for a few bucks." This echoes the way his family was killed for a measly ten dollars. Arthur is comparing himself to their murderers, finally accepting that he failed Eliza and Isaac when he destroyed the Downes family by killing Thomas. He admits, "I've lived a bad life, Sister." Instead of honoring Eliza and Isaac's memory after their death and abandoning his criminal lifestyle, he essentially pretended they never existed by following Dutch's command and living truer to the outlaw code to ease his conscience. But now, because of his tuberculosis, he has a different perspective. He takes responsibility for his actions and rejects the ideology that there is such a thing as an honorable criminal.

This also tells us what he wants from Sister Calderón, a character who is a well-understood symbol of religion, the afterlife, and salvation in general. Arthur wants to confess. He feels an overwhelming sense of guilt, and he doesn't know if he wants redemption or absolution. If Sister Calderón absolves him, she might say, "God and hell are real, and there is nothing a murderous bastard like you can do to save yourself," and then at least he could stop feeling so bad for his sins. The same goes for if she tells him, "God and hell are real, but Jesus already died for your sins, so you have nothing to worry about. Go ahead and live your life, you murderous bastard. Cavort!"

But instead, this is where Sister Calderón teaches Arthur what it truly means to redeem yourself. The irony is, she instructs him not from a religious perspective, but from a secular, human perspective, so it relates to everyone regardless of their beliefs.

Full of surprises, Sister Calderón doesn't blame Arthur or condemn him for his sins. Keep in mind, this woman is a devout member of the church, a servant of God who is literally moments away from leaving on a mission to preach the word. She doesn't tell a confessed robber and murderer he's going to hell for eternity. Instead, she commiserates, reassuring him that everyone sins. The only thing she accuses Arthur being guilty of is not knowing himself. This perplexes Arthur, and he asks for clarification. Sister Calderón explains that the Arthur she knows is generous and neighborly. Which is true for her. But if you asked almost anyone else who has had an encounter with Arthur, they would likely have a much different story.

Her kindness actually prompts Arthur to open up and tell her about his life. Perhaps because he is trying to live through past memories in defiance of what little time he has left. "I had a son; he passed away. I had a girl who loved me; I threw that away." Instead of teaching him, she shows him that she is listening and trying to understand what he needs to feel better. She tells him that her husband died, that life is full of pain. "But it is also full of love and beauty."

Arthur groans, as if he isn't in the mood to hear that he should just look on the bright side of life. He's going to die soon, and he regrets most of his life decisions anyway. What good is there looking on the bright side when he can see only darkness? He doesn't find what he is seeking in the conversation, so Arthur asks her what he is supposed to do with the rest of his life.

Sister Calderón first wisely points out that there is a bright side to his misfortune. He should be grateful that, for the first time, he can see his life clearly for what it is. It may sound morbid, or that she is trying a bit too hard, but it is true. His tuberculosis has caused him to reflect on what he did with his agency. Then she answers his question in a surprising way. She tells him, in very simple terms, that helping others makes you really happy.

Arthur sighs and tilts his head in the carefully animated, beautifully acted scene, indicating that he is tired of hearing trotted-out platitudes of do-goodism and wants some kind of revelation that will instantly make him feel better. "But I still don't believe in nothing." It's significant that he says *still*, here. Indicating that he has wondered for some time about whether God is real.

She tells Arthur that sometimes she doesn't believe in God, either. "But then I meet someone like you, and everything makes sense." It makes Arthur laugh. What I don't think he understands about what she is saying here is that when life gets challenging, it can be easy to forget to help other people. But when she meets someone who is going through a tough time, like Arthur, life makes sense again because she can help them.

Being able to write from different perspectives is a valuable skill for writers, and *Red Dead Redemption II* is expressing that here. From Arthur's point of view, he's looking for Sister Calderón to relieve his pain. From Sister Calderón's point of view, she is also using this opportunity to help Arthur to relieve *her* pain.

Arthur tells her he's afraid. She tells him there is nothing to be afraid of. She reiterates, "Take a gamble that love exists, and do a loving act." This speaks to me. To me, she is saying there is no deep, secret truth about the universe that answers all our greatest questions. Where did we come from? What happens when we die? What is the purpose of life? Her advice is simple, even if it is difficult to put it into practice at times. And there isn't a lot to read into her advice that we haven't discussed already. Do good for the sake of doing good.

This conversation resonated because I am also afraid of what the future holds. Life is full of pain. It's tragic and unfair. Good people die too young, and it feels like the bad guys always win. And not a day goes by that I'm not haunted by my deepest regrets. Just like with any great work of art, Arthur's story expressed my greatest questions, fears, and concerns. And when I felt as hopeless as he did at this point, Sister Calderón gave me hope.

We only have so much power to change the world around us. And so what if there isn't an afterlife? Those are not things you should be afraid of. Why not make what we know *is* real, this life, a better place? And you don't need to pay someone to tell you that you feel happier when you help someone. The reward is in the action itself. It's intrinsic.

The most important part of this game, the part that delivers the theme, is illustrated in this conversation with Sister Calderón. The incredible thing was, after this conversation, I actually felt compelled to do the right thing. In a video game. In a virtual world that doesn't exist—I didn't even have the disc to prove it was real since I installed the game digitally. Still, I wanted to help people along Arthur's journey. I wanted to exercise control over parts of the world I could influence for good. And you can't do that in a book or a movie. You can only tell this kind of story in a video game. And best yet, digitally doing good in the game inspired me to do the same for the people I loved in real life.

Back in the game, Arthur arrives in camp where Leopold Strauss gives him a list of a few more people to strong-arm into repaying their debts to the gang. The interesting thing about this part of the game is, now when the player goes to collect their dues, they have the option to instead forgive their debts and give them money out of Arthur's own pocket. It's like after the conversation with Sister Calderón, the game opens up more opportunities for Arthur to be charitable.

Once Arthur completes his chores for Leopold, he goes back to camp and kicks the loan shark out of the Dutch Boys, the man who first preyed on the Downes family. Arthur remarks that he should have done it a long time ago.

At this point, my mind was made up. I was going to finish the game as honorably as possible. But just to keep things real, I played again at a later date with the opposite in mind and it just didn't feel right. Still, no judgment. The game is literally here for you to take your version of Arthur down the path you think you'll enjoy most, but for me, it was all about redemption.

I decided to put what Sister Calderón taught into practice and try to find some peace for Arthur. And it seems like fate wanted to present me with the perfect opportunity to redeem Arthur as well. On his way returning to camp from the train station, he catches a glimpse of a woman he recognizes. Upon closer inspection, he identifies her as Edith Downes, the wife of the man he beat to death, Thomas Downes. Desperate and destitute, Edith turned to prostitution and Archie, their son, got a job at the mine, where he is being worked to death. Arthur wants to help Edith, but he doesn't know how. He engages conversation with her awkwardly, and she clearly does not want to speak with him. Arthur tries to absolve himself by telling her the world is man unleashed, and she retorts with, "Man unleashed? Then unleash goodness, not just hell's feeble brother, sir."

Finding little inroads to conversation with Mrs. Downes, Arthur goes to the mine to find Archie, who is being picked on by the foreman. Arthur beats the foreman and takes Archie back to his mother. In the meantime, Edith ran off with a customer with a nasty reputation into the woods. Arthur rides after her and threatens the lecherous drunk before he can harm Edith. Arthur gives her a ride back to her son and tries to give them money to get out of town and start a new life. Edith won't accept it. At this point, I didn't feel like Edith was willing to forgive Arthur. But in my mind, that was fine. I didn't want forgiveness for Arthur; I wanted him to truly change. Absolution, or a totally clean slate, wasn't the goal; he just wants to help out a few folks. Reluctantly, Edith accepts the cash, and Arthur returns to camp.

If you've decided to walk the path for redemption, Arthur gets a chance to perform a final loving act as he helps Abigail, Jack, and John Marston escape the gang. Dutch at this point only sees red, and Arthur has completely divorced himself from his surrogate father's will. And Dutch's final big haul puts everyone in the gang who hasn't already left or died because of Dutch at great risk. Instead of following orders, Arthur helps the small family evade the law and Dutch's ire. His reasoning is that he believes there is still love in the world because of the compassion he sees Abigail has for Jack. He pleads with John to make things work for his family and to live an honest life. Before sending them on his way, he gives John his hat and his journal. Then he pulls out his revolver and returns to face Dutch and his selfish batch of cronies.

If you don't have enough honor, then Arthur is executed and doesn't believe he deserves forgiveness. However, if the player has high enough honor, in his final blaze of glory, Arthur dies fighting, believing he tried his best to live a good life in the end. In my mind, the story is at its best when the player dies with honor as high as possible, because it means that Arthur has come full circle and truly learned his lesson. He's redeemed himself for living contrary to his true beliefs, by sacrificing himself for Abigail, Jack, and John. He's also learned that he shouldn't be afraid of dying, because he did his best to serve others. And even if the bad guys get what they want in the end, even if life dealt him a horrible hand, even if he did bad things, even if Eliza and Isaac died unfairly, all that matters to Arthur is that he took a chance that love existed and did a loving act.

In the end, Arthur acknowledges that men do have a knowledge of good and evil and should be responsible for what they do in their lives according to their conscience. Thankfully for him, even though he only has a little time left, his efforts aren't too little, nor too late. Even the smallest gesture of goodwill counts, even if it is the tiniest glimmer of light in a life full of darkness. And while absolution for all the things we regret in our lives might not be possible, there might just be a shot at redemption if we are willing to look for it.

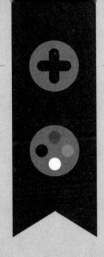

BOOK REPORT:

Mass Effect 2

Mass Effect 2 © BioWare

INITIAL RELEASE DATE AND PLATFORM:

January 2010 for Microsoft Windows, Xbox 360, PlayStation 3

WHERE ELSE CAN IT BE FOUND?

The Legendary Edition (February 2021) can be played on Windows PC, Xbox One, PS4, Xbox Series X, and the PlayStation 5.

CATEGORY:

Linear Narrative, Third-Person Sci-Fi Shooter

MAIN CHARACTERS:

Commander Shepard, the protagonist of the story. A valiant and dedicated person, whose first name, gender, and race are all determined by the player.

Grunt, a genetically engineered Krogan super soldier who fights alongside Commander Shepard.

Miranda Lawson, a human Cerberus Officer and potential romantic interest for Commander Shepard. Miranda is a wellspring of knowledge, being that she is so well traveled and has a vast network of contacts within the Citadel.

Jacob Taylor, a human biotic, former Alliance Marine, and a part of Commander Shepard's squad during the suicide mission.

SETTING:

This game and series are so massive that it's difficult to pin down a few examples of where this game is set. It's in the future, the twenty-second century to be more specific, and it takes place within the Milky Way galaxy, but that is just the beginning. The interiors of hulking ships like the *SSV Normandy*, and the *Normandy SR-2*, the surface of many hostile planets, and sprawling high-tech cities each play a big part in the sci-fi narrative that has garnered scores of dedicated *Mass Effect* fans.

STORY SUMMARY:

The game opens with Shepard's death. Their ship, the *Normandy*, is destroyed by an unknown alien spaceship. Most of the crew survives, but Shepard is lost. Their body is eventually retrieved by a shady human organization called Cerberus. A couple of years later, Cerberus sends Shepard on a mission to find out why human colonies have started disappearing. During their investigation, they discover that the same alien species that attacked the *Normandy*, a group known as the Collectors, is responsible for the loss of the colonies. To face this threat,

Shepard must reassemble their squad of teammates from the first *Mass Effect* game (along with a few new recruits), while also making the proper preparations necessary to commit to a suicide mission on the Collectors' home world with at least a small chance of survival.

WHAT DID YOU THINK OF THIS STORY?

When you have a revered series like *Mass Effect*, it's difficult to pick a favorite. While I love all three of these games, the time spent developing the characters and their relationships really pays off as they are put at risk. *Mass Effect 2* is a great example of a series carrying on and having impact. Important decisions you made in the first game carry over into this one, and many of the choices you make in this game are remembered in the third installment and affect the story. There was a lot of controversy surrounding the ending of the series, but there's no doubt Commander Shepard has a spot in the hearts of many video game story lovers.

Part of this has to do with the way you are able to put yourself into the game as Commander Shepard with the game's create-a-player system. It removes the silent protagonist issue that we see in a lot of first-person shooter games, and brings you in close behind your character in a third-person, over the shoulder, point of view. But it is the literal hours of cinematic quality cut scenes that really help the player attach to the characters in this game. The writing is solid, the voice acting is great, and the hours you spent detailing your Commander Shepard character pay off as you see them come to life on the screen.

Get Inside the Hero's Head

I remember long ago watching my young sons playing with Bionicles, an ancient relic of the toy past. Bionicles are these awesome, posable, customizable action toy figures from Lego. They were kind of like Transformers meet Avatar the Last Airbender, but you could pull them apart to their basic building components and combine them with one another to make something totally new and imaginative. As they were playing, I realized they loved building mechanical warriors with flaming swords and laser eyes because they wanted to *be* them. A similar thing happened when my kids read Harry Potter and anxiously waited for their Hogwarts letter to arrive when they turned eleven. And I recognized it in myself while I played *Red Dead Redemption II* and started talking like a cowboy around the house.

PART OF WHAT MAKES FANTASY SO APPEALING IS that it's an escape from our everyday lives. But in video games, you can be an outlaw roaming the Wild West in *Red Dead Redemption II*. In *The Last of Us*, you can finally test your grit against the zombie apocalypse. *God of War* is the ultimate power trip: Display unbelievable feats of strength in battles with the gods of Norse mythology. Stories are a way to envision what it would be like to explore a new world.

This isn't just a game thing, either. Each storytelling medium has its plusses and minuses. Books are amazing at delivering all the details to the reader exactly as the author intended, while the lack of audio and video can inspire the reader to really push their imagination. Film uses its passive entertainment nature to pull us through a directed, tailored experience, controlling everything from timing to emotional impact. And comics kind of bridge the gap between the two by offering visuals while still controlling the timing of every page turn to surprise the reader with well-placed reveals. There are so many unique forms of storytelling, it's impossible to agree on one that will stand supreme. Each has its own place and does things differently.

Do we have an answer as to what is scientifically the most immersive? I can't say if video games are more or less immersive than other forms of storytelling because of their interactivity. But what I can say is that regardless of the medium, if your story doesn't hold up, it doesn't matter.

Survival in this world is tough. Okay, maybe not so much for us today. If you're hungry, you can pop on over to the grocery store and grab a box of your favorite sugary cereal. For our ancestors, making it through to the next day was a riskier prospect. Stories evolved as a way to simulate experiences through a filter, a protagonist, to learn from. To try to understand how their experiences changed them. Over time, as society and technology advanced, we slowly installed infrastructure that provided creature comforts and amenities that gave us cushy, plush lives. But just because we had to learn how to use a thermostat instead of flint and steel to keep warm doesn't mean stories became irrelevant. If anything, as warnings of physical danger became less relevant, and invisible social dangers became our new predator, they became even more important.

Stories have a greater purpose than simply entertaining us. A flitting fancy that tickles the brain for a moment before wisping away like a puff of smoke. Good stories, where the events have meaning to the protagonist, who changes along a conflicted journey and reaches a concrete resolution, actually have the power to change us.

When technology advanced, stories advanced, too. They adapted to our circumstances and became vehicles to help people navigate difficult social problems, societal ills, morality issues, as well as keep us on our toes physically. I'm looking at you, zombie movies. Stories moved from cautionary tales to a more complex idea allowing us to enter a unique worldview.

If you are reading a book, or hearing a story, or watching a movie, you inhabit the worldview of the protagonist. More than that, even. Neurologically, the parts of the brain that are active while in the throes of an epic tale are that of a participant, not an observer. Which is fascinating, because it means while you are experiencing a story you are compelled to complete, you see yourself as the protagonist. It actually makes sense. If stories evolved as a way to teach us, then it would be much more personal if we could fool ourselves into experiencing the events in the story as if they were our own. It's why it is so enticing to envision yourself as a cowboy in *Red Dead Redemption II* or as a sword- and shield-wielding hero in the *Zelda* franchise. But it becomes emotional when the events that occur to the protagonist are meaningful to them because they are meaningful to us.

The media we choose is important, not only because it keeps us entertained, but because for a short time we get to walk in someone else's shoes. Or better yet, get inside the hero's head. And in a time when we communicate globally at near the speed of light, when we can interface daily with people far outside our normal social circle, at a time when empathy is more needed than any other time in the history of humankind, perhaps we need stories now more than ever.

BOOK REPORT:

Firewatch

Firewatch © Campo Santo

INITIAL RELEASE DATE AND PLATFORM:

February 2016 for Windows PC, PlayStation 4, Windows, Linux, and Mac

WHERE ELSE CAN IT BE FOUND?

Since its release, *Firewatch* has also made its way to the Xbox One and the Nintendo Switch.

CATEGORY:

Linear Narrative, First-Person Storytelling Experience

MAIN CHARACTERS:

Henry, the main protagonist of the story, a somewhat tragic figure rocked with a past filled with lost love, who seeks a new start in the solitude of the Wyoming wilderness.

Delilah, Henry's supervisor, who we meet through conversations over a two-way radio with Henry as the two build up a trusting friendship.

SETTING:

Much can be, and has been, said about the visual style of this game. And while visuals are not necessarily setting, in this case they are worth mentioning. The unique art style of flat shapes and atmosphere landscapes give this game a clean but somehow lonely look that captivated gamers months before the game was released.

You play as a new member of the Firewatch, a group of foresters dotted miles apart in the Wyoming wilderness. The landscape is as harsh and unforgiving as it is peaceful and beautiful, a wonderful contrast and complement to a story that could be defined in the same terms.

STORY SUMMARY:

Firewatch is a mystery set in the Wyoming wilderness, where your only emotional lifeline is the person on the other end of a handheld radio.

Your character, Henry, is working as a fire lookout. Deep in the wilderness, atop a mountain, he can take a break from his complicated life back home and focus on keeping an eye out for smoke. His only human contact is Delilah, his supervisor, who he communicates with via radio.

But one day, Henry notices something strange and has to leave his lookout tower to investigate. Exploring the new wild environment, Henry has to make choices that will forever change the only important relationship he has left, with a woman he will never meet.

WHAT DID YOU THINK OF THIS STORY?

This game is filled with unknowns, packed with strange lore, and overflowing with opportunities to add your own emotions into the mix. While the story is linear and fairly direct, it left an impression on me that inspired me to be more present in my everyday life and personal relationships. Oh, and to spend more time in the woods, too.

Firewatch takes on extremely adult topics like love and loss, alcoholism and dependences on addictions, and the importance of finding connections with others. Its slow place might not be for everyone, but for me it fit perfectly with the flat tone and study-worthy vistas the game offered. The game gives you challenging subjects, but it also offers you plenty of time to reflect. To process. To internalize the importance of being part of something bigger than yourself, even if it only means offering friendship to someone equally lonely and distraught as yourself.

Sure, this sounds heavy and a bit depressing, but the game leaves you on an amazing note of hope. A moment of pure rescue, both literally and metaphorically, as you leave your post in the wilderness and soar off into the sky in hopes of finding a path toward something better.

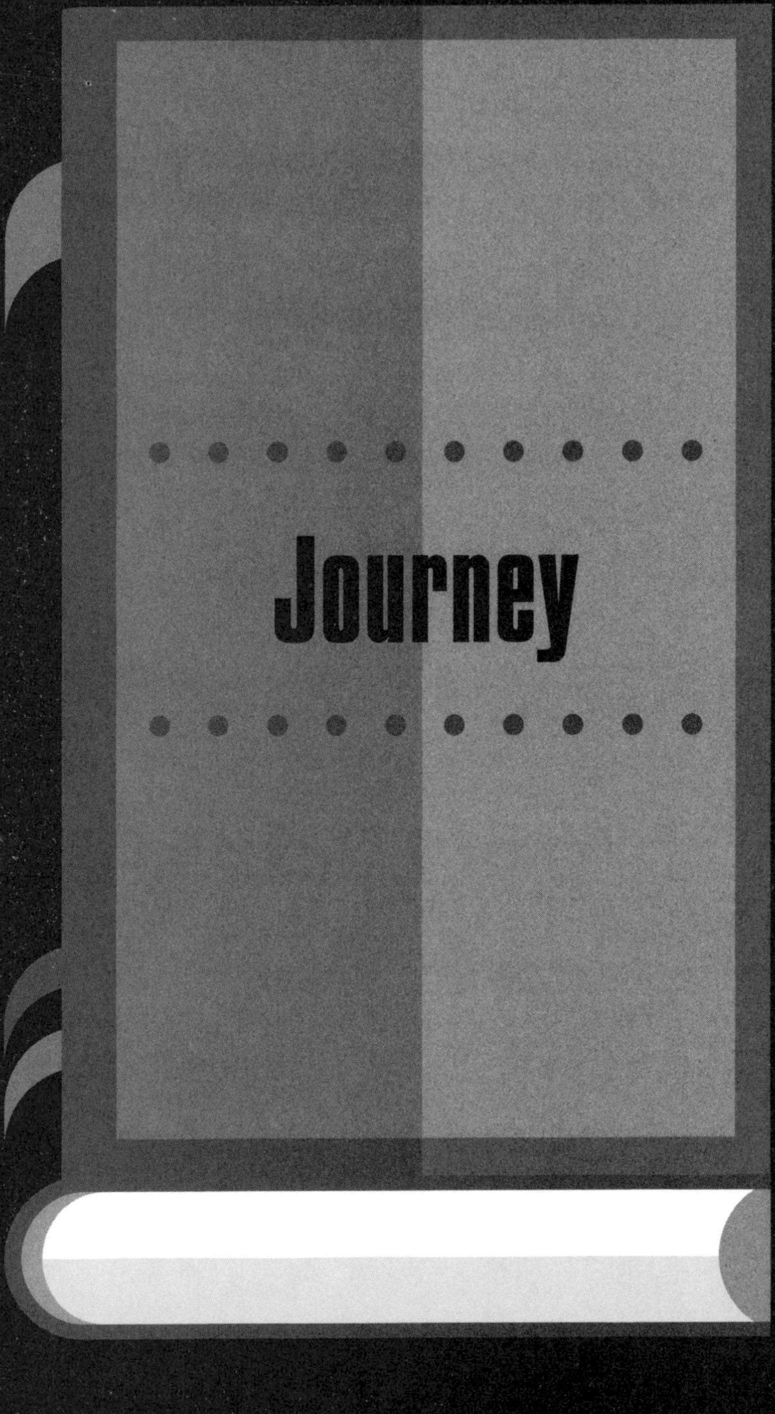
Journey

Contrast (N.)

Contrast is a rhetorical device through which writers identify differences between two subjects, places, persons, things, or ideas. Simply, it is a type of opposition between two objects, highlighted to emphasize their differences.

N THE EARLY DAYS, STORY GAMES MOSTLY INVOLVED huge blocks of text. You may have played some of the early text adventure games like *Zork*, *Planetfall*, or the game adaptation of *The Hitchhiker's Guide to the Galaxy*. They were engrossing, long narratives, with visuals that only existed in the player's imagination. These games are still around today in many forms and formats, including on your phone if you're interested. They are rich, detailed, living novels that offer choice and chance. As you might be able to tell, I'm a fan of the genre, but like the rest of the world, I'm tempted by compelling visuals as well.

In an evolutionary step, many years ago smart developers like Sierra Entertainment added images to this text adventure idea, giving birth to the graphic adventure genre. Games like the *King's Quest* series became instant classics, and they still hold up pretty darn well today. In these games, players were still required to read blocks of text, but instead of adding detailed descriptions of your surroundings in text, characters and the game world were visually displayed on screen. Gamers were giddy, and soon major players like Lucas Arts played along and gave birth to some of the most long-standing and well-loved story games, like the *Monkey Island* series.

Now we no longer had to imagine what Guybrush Threepwood and Elaine Marley, the main characters in the *Monkey Island* games, looked like. We could see Guybrush's golden ponytail and pointy chin. Okay, he was still a bit cartoony and pixelated, but it felt like a step in the right direction.

Then, with the advent of the CD-ROM, games were able to include stereo-quality audio and provide voice acting. Instead of the gamer having to intuit the inflection and emotions of the dialogue, we began to recognize the characters' voices, giving even more personality to the game characters we grew to love. Our shared experience of "It's-a-me, Mario" is an example of this. I'm sure a very high percentage of readers who just read that line heard it in the voice of the beloved plumber himself.

At this point, those large blocks of text moved mainly to menus and side quest information. Especially as developers started using more graphical symbols to express complex concepts in games. *Duke Nukem* gave us the in-world pickup mechanic, simplifying the process even more. If you needed ammo, you had to search through the world until you found an icon of an ammo clip, but then you simply ran over it and ammo appeared in your HUD (heads-up display). No reading, no discussions, no purchasing. Same holds with health pickups, speed boosts, etc.

These iconic images have actually become such a part of the video game landscape that they've moved from being symbolism into a visual gaming language. The study of these signs and symbols is called semiotics, and at this point, it has taken over to the point where reading actual words has all but vanished in most games.

More than once I've walked in on one of my kids playing a game on the PS4 and my first reaction is, what are you watching, not what are you playing. Games are creeping closer and closer to reality. The faces we see in *The Last of Us 2* were modeled after actual people, and those people have gained a sort of celebrity as their faces are being recognized in the real world because of their digital counterparts. And while getting closer to reality is compelling, it also has an interesting downside. The closer we get to feeling like the characters we're playing as are unique, defined people, the more difficult it is to see ourselves in their likeness.

It's a concept a hero of mine, Scott McCloud, points out in his amazing book, *Understanding Comics*. He describes this idea in a different way. Scott shows a graph that goes from a detailed photograph of a man's face to a drawing of the same face, to an abstracted, simplified drawing of the face, and finally to an emoji-style icon of a face. The graph switches from images to language, where it simply states the word *face*, then "two eyes, one nose, mouth," then the more descriptive "the youth's proud livery, so gaz'd on now . . ."

This concept really strikes me at the core. If we look at this from the left (photo of a man) to the right (complex description of a man), we move from the received to the perceived. In other words, the closer we get to visual reality, the more we receive all the visual information we need and leave very little up to interpretation. To the far right of the graph, we get a written, detailed description that asks us to fill in what we read with memories or relatable images from our imagination, but still, it's very unambiguous and limits what we imagine.

In the center, with the emoji and the word *face*, we are left with plenty of room for inserting our own experiences. When I see an emoji or a simplified drawing of a face, I might interpret it as myself or a loved one. You would undoubtedly do the same, but they will both be very different in our internal perception. And every interpretation would be correct.

It seems as though I'm going on a tangent here, but it really is the crux of what makes a game like *Journey* special. Voice acting, writing, text, detail . . . all those things are washed away and replaced by symbols we recognize but can't quite identify. If you were to place this game on Scott McCloud's reception/perception graph, it would live in the center, which encourages us to add our own experience, our own imagination, and most important, our own interpretation into the game.

Of course, this means that when it comes to describing the story of *Journey*, my take will be different from yours. Just as if we were to compare our unique interpretations of the smiley face emoji. Similar in subject, very different in emotional impact and takeaway. But . . . I'm going to try, because I think it is one of the most important examples of how this new medium, video games, can ask us how to participate in story.

Journey begins by introducing you to a cloaked figure, with a dark, nondescript face and two glowing eyes. No names are given, nor tales told, as the camera swings around behind the cloaked figure and you are given control. With the most minimal instruction given, you are encouraged to move the joystick, and the cloaked figure responds. The open desert you find yourself in is warm and barren. Pillars of stone rise from rolling sand hills, and off in the near distance, a squarish, dark platform is visible, partly buried in the sand. No narrators chime in to direct you. Only curiosity and the human desire to discover lead you toward the platform, nothing more.

Journey © thatgamecompany

Once you climb up on the platform, you receive the most important instruction you'll need for this experience, to "sing" spells itself out in the sky. Your voice, a simple chime, rings at the press of a button, and scraps of cloth seem to awaken as they float around you. White icons, familiar but unrecognizable, glow on the surface of the cloth, then fade away to reveal a seemingly ancient language.

That's all you need to know for your journey. Walk, jump, and sing. Some games try to pad in as many varieties of gameplay functionality as possible, but not this one. *Journey* knows its purpose and gives players as few distractions as possible from it. After the briefest of tutorials, the player is encouraged to let their curiosity guide them through this visual song. Somehow, this intentionally handcrafted, linear experience feels open and free. If you so choose, you could simply wander around in the desert for hours. It would be easy to assign meaning to this metaphor, but I'll leave that up to you when you try this game out on your own.

While floating gracefully through rolling hills of pink sand is interesting at first, eventually I wanted something else to do. The only outstanding landmark is a massive mountain on the horizon, and I felt drawn to it. This first level set the pattern for navigation for the rest of the game as my eyes were drawn to this geometric monolith in the soft, rolling landscape.

It all comes down to contrast. *Journey* uses a method of designing visual points of interest to pop out on the landscape to guide the player to the next destination. If you remember back when we were talking about plot, I said that it was a series of events, where one influences the next. Well, in this case, contrasting visual design (dark objects on a light background; sharp, mechanical objects paired against sloping hills of sand; etc. . . . .) drives the plot of the game. Distant indicators catch the player's eye and promise an evolution in the story at their location. It is fantastic level design. The unique set pieces are like breadcrumbs sprinkled throughout the ancient desert topography.

Relying on the principle of contrast to guide your curiosity, to make the sparse wasteland feel more alive, the world slowly introduces players to never before explored life. Subverting expectations of what an expansive dust bowl is supposed to be like. Flying creatures, made from the same cloth you awakened earlier, enjoy your company. They aren't afraid or worried. They seem to want to be near you as they spirit through the air with grace and lead you to abandoned buildings and structures half-buried in the sand, which hint to a former advanced civilization. Not coincidentally, your free-willed exploration aligns with the game's designated linear path, thanks to the exceptionally directed visual design.

The game is void of traditional gaming devices. You don't have a health bar to tell you if your cloaked persona is surviving. You don't have an XP score or additional abilities you need to learn to move on. There is no minimap at the bottom that flashes your next quest, you simply wander, drawn along by interest and wonder. The closest thing to an in-game user interface is a meter that shows you how long you can glide through the air after a jump. But even this is built into the runes and glyphs written on the cape and ribbon you wear, allowing you to leave your full focus on the character you have become.

Journey © *thatgamecompany*

One of the most defining and impressive features of *Journey* is its ability to show us scale. It's common in video games, like *God of War,* to make the player feel powerful. But in *Journey,* it felt to me like the opposite. I felt small. And while I had this strange ability to awaken the world by singing into the glyphs and tapestries, I was constantly reminded of my place within this experience. Such a small creature in what feels like a nearly infinite world. The world-building is so beautifully done, with ancient ruins half-buried in the sand and glyphs left behind by a long-gone civilization, that I had the impression I was nothing more than a blip on the time line of a story that goes back for eons. The notes I sang to interact with the world blended in with a complex and rich musical landscape to a point where I was nothing more than a single thread in that aural tapestry. And I was reminded as I met others in the game that even they were a small fraction of the billions of beings in existence, before and after our time within the game. This sense of scale fills my mind with something I can only call awe, which has honestly never been matched for me in any other medium. Period.

Another brilliant aspect of this game is how it is edited down to its very essence. We live in a time when video game consoles have the power to add details like moss growing on rocks, and I do mean literally growing as time passes. We can see players in a sports game progressively get covered in mud and grass stains and decorated with crystal jewels of sweat. But in contrast, that-gamecompany took a minimalist approach to *Journey.* Everything from the soundscape to the visuals to the gameplay mechanics are reduced to only their most important features. Sparse, yet perfect. I mentioned there were only a few mechanics, walking, jumping, and singing, which seems extreme, but even that wasn't entirely accurate. Jumping happens automatically as you climb through rough terrain. The jumping I was referring to earlier is actually more like flying or gliding, but the controls are so smooth between walking and skating in the sand that flying almost feels like an extension of the same mechanic. To describe the motion in *Journey*, you might need to say the character walk/glide/skate/fly/float/skim/scrapes around the environment, which is a mouthful. Especially considering the game handles the transition between all these movement styles seamlessly without asking you to choose between them. It's almost as if it plays itself. All the player needs to do is point in the direction they want to go.

It's kind of back to the original point I was trying to make. By removing everything concrete and definitive, *Journey* has provided us more with less. Design by subtraction, asking us to create story out of context and experience, not narrative.

But there *is* narrative. Generally, you begin wandering, alone, in this multiplayer experience. If you happen upon another traveler, you can communicate with them with your singing. Single notes, similar but not identical to one another, that càn be shared in this musical way; haunting, yet somehow connective.

Journey © thatgamecompany

Later in your journey, you find some ruins, large and foreboding, with torn, wordless banners stretching between them. As you fly to these massive stone pillars and share your life-giving voice with the old cloth, it takes form as the glowing runes light up and the cloth becomes a bridge. You use these bridges to move from the beginning, wandering portion of the game to one of the most freeing and happy experiences. I wish I had another word for this, but that's just what it is. Happy.

The music picks up speed as you glide freely down enormous mountains of sand. Other creatures dance and swirl around you as you play in this abandoned yard, joyriding through this moment of bliss. For me, it brought back memories of riding my BMX bike down Ephraim Canyon Road in my hometown, no helmet (it was the mid-1970s, we didn't really have such things back then), no shirt, no hands on the handlebars. The wind feathered my hair as I flapped, as free as a bird, and zoomed down the old, paved road, careless and happy. As happy as I can ever remember.

Blindly, you follow the path of this winding happiness until you are launched into the air, and when you fall, you fall hard and deep. The color in the world dramatically shifts from oranges and golds to blues and grays. For me, I could almost feel the temperature in the room drop as I stood, suddenly alone, at the bottom of a pit so deep that for the first time I had lost sight of the mountain that had been my internal compass since the opening minutes of the game.

The stark contrast from reckless happiness to lonely despair felt palpable to me. The music, which almost seemed to paint its own warm hues earlier, abandoned me. Silent, except for the sound of footsteps as I moved forward, unsure for the first time where I needed to go.

While there are no words inside *Journey*, the most direct example of narrative comes in the form of wall art. Inside rooms and caves, the game unfurls stylized paintings that seem to unwrap as you discover them. I won't go into what these paintings suggest because I don't think my interpretation matters, yours does. But I will say that it seems as though thatgamecompany is leaning on an amalgamation of multiple religious themes and legends that have a way of resonating with just about everyone. I found the story remarkably personal. I will also say this: The stories found on the walls, the cave paintings as some have called them, are mostly backstory. They add depth and context to the ruins and abandoned cities that you've been journeying through. But they also mark some of the momentous points in your current experience. You see yourself, the cloaked figure, drawn on the walls, and this gives the game, and the visual story it tells, a prophetic feeling.

The story told in the cave paintings converges with your own experience even more as you are presented with the almost insurmountable task of climbing to the top of the very mountain that has been your guide for so long. You find yourself at the foot of this monolith, and snow begins to fall. The music builds to a strong crescendo as you leave behind the gliding, jumping, soaring joy and replace it with walking/struggling/climbing. You've been aiming for this mountain, for this final meeting between your journey and your destiny, for the entire game. It really shouldn't be a surprise that it is difficult, yet it still packs an emotional punch. You move slower in the deep snow, and the wind pushes you back. Movement is more work. You can't even slide down the slopes anymore, being forced instead to carefully plan your path down the rare areas you move downhill for a few steps. It's not that the gameplay is more challenging mechanically. Rather, it feels more demanding because your hindered movement is much slower in comparison with the freedom in the beginning.

As you reach the pinnacle of the mountain, the struggle to move forward becomes more than you can maintain. For me, I didn't have time to reflect on the good moments in the game, I was too consumed with an overwhelming feeling that I wasn't going to reach the top. I was close, but I could tell both the game itself, and my cloaked figure, had had enough.

The ending, and perhaps new beginning, of *Journey* is such a singular experience that I'm going to stop right now. Perhaps I've already said too much. I've played through this game many times. Each experience offers a little more, a little something different. Sometimes my journey to the light in the mountain is solo from start to finish and I'm able to be more introspective about my response to the experience. Other times, I've been joined by other players, actual people who I don't know in the real world. Other travelers on a similar path. I've been grateful for their company, and honestly sorrowful when we part.

In the end, I'm not sure I really understand this game. I'm not sure I ever will. Maybe, someday, who knows. Honestly, I don't think it matters if I do. For me, what matters most is that for a few hours, when I let myself fall into this powerful story, I can stand in awe of the journey, and that is enough.

The Beginning

Conclusion (N.)

The final summation of a trial of strength or skill. The end or finish of an event in process; a judgment or decision reached by reasoning.

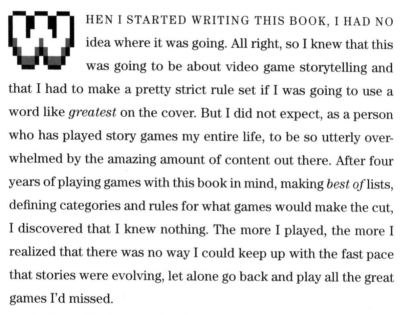HEN I STARTED WRITING THIS BOOK, I HAD NO idea where it was going. All right, so I knew that this was going to be about video game storytelling and that I had to make a pretty strict rule set if I was going to use a word like *greatest* on the cover. But I did not expect, as a person who has played story games my entire life, to be so utterly overwhelmed by the amazing amount of content out there. After four years of playing games with this book in mind, making *best of* lists, defining categories and rules for what games would make the cut, I discovered that I knew nothing. The more I played, the more I realized that there was no way I could keep up with the fast pace that stories were evolving, let alone go back and play all the great games I'd missed.

But then, I had a singular thought. Sure, these are the greatest stories ever played, but greatest doesn't have to be the end.

If these greatest games stand on the shoulders of the good, then it only makes sense that these great games will become the pillars of what comes next. So I leave it with you now, gamer. Or maybe you're a designer? An author? A storyteller? A story lover? All the above? Regardless, I leave you with this one last question, and it's a biggie. Don't let me down.

What comes after great?

GLOSSARY OF TERMS

|||||||||||||||||||||||||||||||||||||||||||||||||||||||||||||||||||||||||||||||||||||||||||||||||||||||||||||||||||||||||||||||||

Antagonist

A person who is opposed to, struggles against, or competes with another. An opponent, an adversary. The adversary of the hero or protagonist of a drama or other literary work.

Archetype (archetypal)

The original pattern or model from which all things of the same kind are copied or on which they are based.

In literary criticism, those images, figures, character types, settings, and story patterns that, according to Swiss analytical psychologist Carl Jung, are universally shared by people across cultures.

Backstory

A backstory, background story, or background is a set of events invented for a plot, presented as preceding and leading up to that plot. It is a literary device of a narrative history all chronologically earlier than the narrative of primary interest.

Bullet hell

A subgenre of shooters whose main gameplay focus is dodging seemingly endless waves of incoming bullets. In these games, the player controls a small ship or character that flies around the environment, dodging and shooting at waves of enemies to stay alive.

Chiasmus

A reversal in the order of words in two otherwise parallel phrases, as in "He went to the country, to the town went he." Latin for cross, this can also refer to a more global switch of two story elements, with a centralized point where the two collide.

Colloquialism

A style of writing that conveys the effect of informal spoken language as distinct from formal or literary English.

The use of informal words, phrases, or even slang in a piece of writing.

Contrast

A rhetorical device through which writers identify differences between two subjects, places, persons, things, or ideas. Simply, it is a type of opposition between two objects, highlighted to emphasize their differences.

Denouement

The resolution of a plot that occurs after its climax. Denouement is not a literary technique; rather, it is one of several literary terms that describe a plotted conflict's unfolding and resolution.

Deuteragonist

From the Greek *deuteragōnistēs*, for "second actor," a deuteragonist is the second-most important and present character in a story—often called a secondary main character.

Directed game

A directed game is commonly linear in nature. It contains obstacles that must be overcome to progress toward a resolution, but the choices for narrative agency are limited and directed by the game itself, not the player.

Dramatic irony

A literary device by which the audience's or reader's understanding of events or individuals in a work surpasses that of its characters. Dramatic irony is a form of irony that is expressed through a work's structure: An audience's awareness of the situation in which a work's characters exist differs substantially from that of the characters', thus the words and actions of the characters take on a different—often contradictory—meaning for the audience than they have for the work's characters.

Figurative language

Figurative language uses figures of speech to be more effective, persuasive, and have impact. Figures of speech, such as metaphors, similes, and allusions, go beyond the literal meanings of the words to give readers new insights. On the other hand, alliterations, imageries, or onomatopoeias are figurative devices that appeal to the senses of the readers.

First-person game

In video games, first person is any graphical perspective rendered from the viewpoint of the player's character, or a viewpoint from the cockpit or front seat of a vehicle driven by the character. Many genres incorporate first-person perspectives, among them adventure games, driving, sailing, amateur flight simulation, and combat flight simulation. The most notable is the first-person shooter, in which the graphical perspective is an integral component of the gameplay.

First-person narrative

Point of view in fiction simply means who tells the story. In the first-person point of view, a character in the story serves as the narrator, using "I" or "we" as the story plays out.

Foil

Foil is a literary device designed to illustrate or reveal information, traits, values, or motivations of one character through the comparison and contrast of another character. A literary foil character serves the purpose of drawing attention to the qualities of another character, frequently the protagonist. This is effective as a means of developing a deeper understanding of a character by emphasizing their strengths and weaknesses. In addition, a literary foil allows writers to create a counterpart for the protagonist that puts their actions and choices in context.

Foreshadowing

Foreshadowing is a literary device in which a writer gives an advance hint of what is to come later in the story. Foreshadowing often appears at the beginning of a story, or a chapter, and it helps the reader develop expectations about the upcoming events.

Freytag's Pyramid

Devised by nineteenth-century German playwright Gustav Freytag, Freytag's Pyramid is a paradigm of dramatic structure outlining the seven key steps in successful storytelling: exposition, inciting incident, rising action, climax, falling action, resolution, and denouement.

Gameplay

Gameplay is the specific way in which players interact with a game, and in particular with video games. Gameplay is the pattern defined through the game rules, connection between the player and the game, challenges and overcoming them, plot and player's connection with it.

Genre

Genre is any form or type of communication in any mode (written, spoken, digital, artistic, etc.) with socially agreed-upon conventions developed over time.

Genre is most popularly known as a category of literature, music, video games or other forms of art or entertainment, whether written or spoken, audio or visual, based on some set of stylistic criteria, yet genres can be aesthetic, rhetorical, communicative, or functional.

Genres form by conventions that change over time as cultures invent new genres and discontinue the use of old ones. Often, works fit into multiple genres by way of borrowing and recombining these conventions. Stand-alone texts, works, or pieces of communication may have individual styles, but genres are amalgams of these texts based on agreed-upon or socially inferred conventions. In games, some genres may have rigid, strictly adhered-to guidelines, while others may show great flexibility.

Immersive

Noting or relating to digital technology or images that actively engage one's senses and may create an altered mental state, seeming to surround the audience, player, etc. so that they feel completely involved in the content they are interacting with.

In medias res

In medias res means narrating a story from the middle after supposing that the audiences are aware of past events. It is a Latin phrase that literally denotes "in the midst of things." Hence, authors employ this expression as a common strategy to initiate their stories.

In medias res demands beginning a narrative in the very middle of its action from some vital point when most of the action has occurred. The author then freely moves backward and forward at their leisure, connecting the dots of the story. All the explanations regarding the significance of setting, plot, characters, and the minutiae of the story are gradually revealed in the form of a character's dialogue, thoughts, or flashbacks. The setting and environment also contribute to add to the details of the action introduced at the beginning of the story.

Inciting incident

An event or a point that arrives at the beginning of a story that disturbs the actions and life of a protagonist and sets them to pursue the mission vigorously. It originates from a Latin word, *incitāre*, which means to "start up, to put something into rapid motion, or to stimulate, or encourage something or some character."

Internal conflict

A psychological struggle within the mind or heart of a character, often defined as man versus the self, in which the character is required to grow or change to find a satisfying resolution.

Irony

A literary device in which there is a contrast between expectation and reality. For example, the difference between what something appears to mean versus its literal meaning. Irony is associated with both tragedy and humor.

Juxtaposition

Generally speaking, juxtaposition refers to a stark contrast between two people or things. In literature, juxtaposition is a literary device used to create deliberate differences for the reader to compare and contrast.

Linear branching narrative

Linear branching narratives make the participant feel as though they have the power to change story, branching first from point A to point B, C, or D, etc., until you reach the end of your destination.

Linear narrative

A linear story begins on point A and connects through checkpoints in chronological order until point B, where the story ends.

Literal language

Literal language means exactly what it says, while figurative language uses similes, metaphors, hyperbole, and personification to describe something, often through comparison with something different.

Ludo-narrative dissonance

The conflict between a video game's narrative told through the story and the narrative told through the gameplay. Ludo-narrative, a compound of ludology and narrative, refers to the intersection in a video game of ludic elements (gameplay) and narrative elements.

Motif

Motif is a literary technique that consists of a repeated element that has symbolic significance to a literary work. Often in games, a motif is a recurring image, scene, or music theme. The key aspect is that a motif repeats, and through this repetition helps to illuminate the dominant ideas, central themes, and deeper meaning of a story.

Motivation

In literature, "motivation" is defined as a reason behind a character's specific action or behavior. This type of behavior is characterized by the character's own consent and willingness to do something. There are two types of motivation: one is intrinsic (or internal), while the other one is extrinsic (external).

Nonlinear narrative

A nonlinear narrative is when events are portrayed out of the order they actually happen in, such as with flashbacks, distinctive plotlines outside the main story, or parallel narratives.

NPC characters

A nonplayer character (NPC) is any character in a game who is not controlled by a player. The term originated in traditional tabletop role-playing games, where it applies to characters controlled by the game master or referee rather than another player.

Objective

Objective description is primarily factual, omitting any attention to the writer, especially with regard to the writer's feelings. Objective content is empirical and can be proved beyond doubt and voice of emotional context.

Open-world game

An open-world game has obstacles the player must overcome if they want to reach a resolution, but they have a lot of choices to play with before they choose to progress. No defined order is implied, leaving the player the option to explore the world openly, without consequences to the narrative.

Parallel narrative

The term parallel narratives, also referred to as parallel stories or parallel plots, denotes a story structure in which the writer includes two or more separate narratives linked by a common character, event, or theme.

Plot

In a literary work, game, film, or story, the plot is the sequence of events where each affects the next one through the principle of cause and effect. The causal events of a plot can be thought of as a series of events linked by the connector "and so."

Protagonist

Protagonist comes from a Greek word for the "principal actor" in a drama. In modern literature, the protagonist drives the story forward by pursuing a goal. The protagonist of a story is sometimes called the main character and is often opposed by the antagonist.

Real-time strategy

A genre of video games in which a player battles enemies, faces environmental challenges, or achieves a goal while other player characters and nonplayer characters are playing simultaneously, without sequenced turns or rounds of play. Abbreviation: RTS

Sandbox game

A sandbox game is a video game with a gameplay element that gives the player a great degree of creativity to complete tasks toward a goal within the game, if such a goal exists. Some games exist as pure sandbox games with no objectives, conflict, or resolution. These are also known as nongames or software toys.

Second-person narrative

Second-person point of view uses the pronoun "you" to address the reader. This narrative voice implies that the reader is either the protagonist or a character in the story and the events are happening to them.

Semiotics

The study of signs and symbols and their use and interpretation.

Story

A story is when a character faces an unavoidable, challenging obstacle and how they change because of it.

Subjective

Subjective description includes attention to both the subject described and the writer's reactions (internal, personal) to that subject. Reaction to the content is, therefore, interpretive, asking the viewer to draw their own conclusions and impressions.

Subtheme

A secondary, subordinate, or supportive theme in a work of literature.

Symbolism

Symbolism is a literary device that uses symbols, be they words, people, marks, locations, or abstract ideas, to represent something beyond the literal meaning. The concept of symbolism is not confined to works of literature: Symbols inhabit every corner of our daily life.

Theme

A universal idea, lesson, or message explored throughout a work of literature. One key characteristic of literary themes is their universality, which is to say that themes are ideas that not only apply to the specific characters and events of a book or play, but also express broader truths about human experience that readers can apply to their own lives.

Tone

The overall mood or message of a story. It can be established through a variety of means, including characterizations, pace, difficulty, visuals, symbolism, and themes.

Third-person game

In a third-person game, the player's camera view is positioned outside the game character's body, usually from behind or to the side to show character movement and involvement with their surroundings.

Third-person narrative

Any story told in the grammatical third person, i.e., without using "I" or "we."

ACKNOWLEDGMENTS

||||||||||||||||||||||||||||||||||||||||||||||||||||||||||||||||||||||||||||||||||||||||||||||||||||||||||||||

I DON'T KNOW WHERE I'D BE WITHOUT VIDEO GAMES. Back in the day, my parents were bright enough to see that they would take me somewhere, and they surrounded me with tech and opportunities to both play and create in this space. So acknowledging them seems like the right place to start. If it wasn't for the TI-99/4A and games like Scott Adams's *Pirate Adventure* that you put in my hands in 1979, I wouldn't be writing this book today.

As a dyslexic reader who loved story but struggled with reading, I was able to see new ways to tell stories through visuals, games, and comics mostly, so Mom and Dad, thanks for seeing something in me long before I could see it in myself.

Thanks to my constant writing friends. Knowing that you are all typing words late into the night with me gives me strength. I really do love and admire each of you greatly. Jamie Ford, Aprilynne Pike, Margaret Dilloway, Ben Brooks, and Natalia Sylvester, how does Wednesday at noon PST sound?

A million thanks to my wife, Jodi, the first non-gamer to read my book. When she was hooked, I knew I was on the right track. Thanks, Jodi, for constantly pointing me in the right direction, for finding a dump truck full of typos and bad grammar, and for always joining me for a brainstorm soak in the hot tub.

A special thanks needs to go to my little gamers, Tanner, Brynn, Malorie, and Annie. I love you all more than you can imagine, and yes, you all cheat when we play Mario Kart. I know it!

The Greatest Stories Ever Played would not be here without my agent, Gemma Cooper, and a passionate editor, Holly West. I'm grateful to consider you both friends, and after a working on eight books together, that says something. Thanks for believing in this book, and for believing in me.

And to put a final closing bow to this book, I think it's only fair to thank the creators. The game designers, the narrative designers, the artists, producers, engineers, and testers who put their hearts into the games that keep me up at night. What an amazing time to be a storyteller. Thanks for the inspiration and companionship you've all provided, not just to me, but to millions of other hungry gamers out there. We're ready for the next one, and we always will be.

GAME ON!